How To Work For Yourself And Win

by
Ian Rowland

Publication

How To Work For Yourself And Win

by Ian Rowland

1st edition

Copyright © 2020 Ian Rowland. All rights reserved.
ISBN 978 1 916 2408 3 4

Published by Ian Rowland Limited.

Dedication

I dedicate this book to everyone who is self-employed or wants to be.

I also dedicate it to all my amazing, talented self-employed friends around the world. Thank you for all that we have shared, both personally and professionally. It has been quite an adventure!

Let's all help one another to succeed.

A Quick Note About Me

I do three things so I have three websites.

www.ianrowland.com

This is about my work as a professional writer. In simple terms, I offer a complete 'start-to-finish' writing and publishing service. Technical writing, business, sales, marketing, creative... you name it, I've done it! I offer 35+ years experience across all media. In my career, I've helped more companies to sell a greater range of goods and services than anyone else you're likely to meet. I'm also a 'ghostwriter'! If you've got a book inside you, I can write it for you or guide you through the self-publishing process.

- - -

www.coldreadingsuccess.com

My website devoted to the art, science and joy of cold reading and what I call 'cold reading for business'. As well as providing free information and downloads, the site tells you about my three books on cold reading and the training I offer.

- - -

www.ianrowlandtraining.com

All about my talks and training for conferences, corporate groups and private clients. Main subjects include:

- The Practical Persuasion Method.
- Creative Problem-Solving.
- Leadership, Presence And Charisma.
- Unlock Your Mind.
- Be A Genius!
- Cold Reading For Business.

I also offer bespoke training packages to suit *your* needs. Clients to date include the FBI, Google, Coca-Cola, Unilever, the Ministry Of Defence, the British Olympics Team, the Crown Estate and many more. Full details on the site.

About My Books

Different Sites, Different Books

I've written a few books that I sell from my three different websites.

I sell this book mainly from www.ianrowland.com, together with a few other books and some free downloads that are mainly about business and personal development.

On www.coldreadingsuccess.com you'll find three different books about various aspects of cold reading, plus some related information and downloads.

Finally, on www.ianrowlandtraining.com you'll find all my current books in paperback and Kindle form plus some free booklets for instant download.

If you enjoy this book, I hope you'll consider checking out some of my other publications as well!

Please Tell Your Friends

If you want to tell your friends about me and this book, which I hope you will, it helps me if you send them to my own website rather than to the lovely people at Amazon:

www.ianrowland.com

I *have* made this book available on Amazon (paperback only) because these days people think that if a book's not on Amazon it doesn't exist.

However, it's nicer for me if people order from my own website, where you will also find the Kindle version, extra information, free downloads, related products and discount deals not available elsewhere.

So, please direct your friends to me rather than to Amazon if at all possible.

Thank you!

Contents

1. What This Book Is About   **12**

Who This Book Is For   13
A Special Note For Young People   13

2. Changing World, Fewer Jobs   **16**

3. Get Yourself Ready   **20**

Expectations And Attitude   20
Health And Fitness   21
Attitude   22
Invest In Yourself   22
Fall In Love With Commercial Reality   23

4. Get Your Business Set Up   **28**

Find Your Mentor   28
See To The Legal And Accounting Stuff   29
Understand The Financial Basics   30
Your Business Plan   32
Practicalities   32
Don't Get Stuck On Trivia   33
Don't Chase Grants   34
Don't Start Off In A Partnership   34
Don't Think Buying Is Achieving   35
Don't Believe Most Ventures Fail   35
Don't Worry About Constraints   35

5. Get Your Product Right   **38**

Deciding What To Sell   38
What Value Can You Offer?   40
Find The Golden Eagle In You   40
The Product Reality Check   41
One Talent, Many Opportunities   42

6. Shout About It   46

Marketing Basics   46
Quick Guide To Promotion   47

7. About Productivity   52

Organise, Don't Improvise   52
Turn Off TV   55
Avoid The Internot   56
Get Out Of Bed   56
Time-shift Your Attitude   57
Take Time Off   57

8. Dealing With Common Blocks   60

Block #1: Fear   60
Block #2: Self-Pity   62
Block #3: Self-doubt   63
Block #4: Procrastination   66
Block #5: What Other People Might Say   68
Block #6: The Grass Is Always Greener   70

9. Good Things To Do   74

Make Connections   74
Use The Internet   75
Look After Your Body   76
Look After Your Mind   78
Use ABC   80
Dress To Impress   81
Do Some Charity Work   81
Travel As Much As You Can   82

10. Build Your Network   86

Reach Out To People   86
Build Credibility And Respect   87
Don't Judge On Looks   87
Collaboration Is Good   87
Be Good PR For One Another   88
Offer Commission   89
Learn About Other Self-employed Journeys   89

11. Good Principles To Follow   **94**

Small, Simple, Humble   94
Always Try To DIY   96
Connect To Effect: Email, Call, Meet   98
Living For Giving   99
Talk And Listen   100
Yearn To Learn   103
Know Your Tools   105
Build On Success   105
To Get It Right, Get It Written   107

12. Good Values To Have   **110**

Be Reliable   110
Be Honourable   112
Do The Right Thing   113
Be Polite   113
Be Grateful   114
The Attitude Of Gratitude   114
Be Likeable (Rather Than Nice)   115
Under-promise, Over-deliver   115
Have A Sense Of Humour   116

13. Good Ways To Respond   **120**

When People Let You Down   120
When People Treat You Badly   120
When People Don't Believe In You   122
When People Aren't Buying   124
When Plans Go Wrong   125
When An Idea Doesn't Work   126
When You've Got A Problem   127

14. Things To Avoid   **130**

Avoid Atrocious Advice   130
Avoid Granite Trampolines   132
Avoid Time Vampires   133
Don't Work For Nothing   134
Don't Compete On Price   135
Respect The Legalities   136
Be Careful About TV   138

15. Dealing With Criticism · 142

The 10:10:80 Principle · 142
Two Quotations · 143
Learn If You Can, Ignore If You Can't · 143
The Two Dresses Syndrome · 144
Opinion And Judgment · 145
The BITDIG Principle · 146
Goldman's Beautiful Advice · 147

16. About Making Money · 152

Mental Blocks (1) · 152
Mental Blocks (2) · 153
Two Lessons · 154
'Get' Versus 'Allow' · 157
Making And Sticking · 158
A Few More Money Notes · 159
A Note About Advertising · 160
A Note About Agents · 161

17. Success Mythology · 164

Myth #1: Get Rich Quick · 164
Myth #2: Magic Marketing And TABU Tales · 165
Myth #3: Big Numbers · 167
Myth #4: Celebrity Culture · 168

18. Success Reality · 172

Defining Success · 172
Step 1. Believe In Yourself x 4 · 173
Step 2. Have A Clear Goal · 174
Step 3. Pursue One Main Goal · 174
Step 4. Focus Mostly On Effort · 175
Step 5. Spot Opportunities, Take Action · 176
Step 6. Prefer Positive Doing · 177
Step 7. Be Ready For Breaks · 178
Step 8. Be Persistent · 178
Step 9. Smile, Get Up Again · 180
Step 10. Always Learn From Experience · 180

19. Further Thoughts On Success — 182

About Competition — 182
Pride Versus Profit — 184
The Truth About Talent — 184
The Madonna Gardening Book Theory — 185
Success Takes Many Forms — 185
If You Want A Guarantee, Get A Toaster — 186

20. Thoughts To Share — 190

Inspiration #1: Your 'It's Too Late' Day — 190
Inspiration #2: The One Way Wall — 191
Inspiration #3: The Two Tables — 192

21. Changes — 196

Change The World — 196
Change Yourself — 197

22. A Bit About Me — 200

Love And Gratitude — 212

1. What This Book Is About

"To succeed in life, you need three things:
a wishbone, a backbone and a funny bone."

— Reba McEntire

1. What This Book Is About

"I just can't do this anymore."

Twenty-three years ago, sitting at my London office desk job, this thought kept swimming back into my mind. It's not that I had a terrible life. Things were largely okay. However, part of me felt that *maybe* I could find a more satisfying path than being a replaceable cog in a corporate machine making someone else quite wealthy. Call me insanely ambitious but I dared to hope there was a better option out there.

I quit my job and started working for myself.

It's been a rough, tough, great, exhausting, wild, joyful, ecstatic and unbelievably challenging ride. The lows have been a little rough but the highs have made Everest look like a rather small bump by comparison. I'm still here, all these years later, somehow earning a living and loving every dazzling, bewildering, magnificent second of it.

This book doesn't contain fake (but appealing) 'get rich quick' advice, pipe dreams, speculation, wishful thinking or false promises. If that's the kind of thing you want, there's buckets of it available elsewhere.

What these pages *do* contain is more than two decades of practical experience. Take my brain, squeeze and wring it like a wet cloth, collect the drips and this book is what you'd get. It's all practical, useful advice distilled from over two decades of experience and a *lot* of mistakes.

It's not my intention to *persuade* anyone to work for themselves. However, if this is what you want to do, my aim is to give you all the guidance I wish someone had given me when I started out. As soon as I invent a time machine, I'll go back to when I was a teenager and give this book to myself (and some winning lottery numbers).

Welcome to 'How To Work For Yourself And Win'.

Who This Book Is For

If you work for yourself, or want to, this book is for you. To be more specific, I hope it will be read by at least four groups of people:

- People who are currently where I was over twenty years ago. You have a job but you know there's no such thing as job security any more so you're exploring your options. Also, you feel a bit unfulfilled and want to do more with your life than just work for someone else every day.

- Young people who haven't yet found their direction but feel inclined towards self-employment.

- PACE people: Performers, Artists, Creative people and Esoteric. In other words, people with slightly unusual talents and ambitions who don't suit conventional career paths.

- Parents and friends of anyone in the above three groups. You want to help but you're not sure how.

I hope this book can fill some gaps, light a few fires of ambition and help one or two people to realise their dreams.

A Special Note For Young People

If you're a young person trying to decide what to do with your life, you know it's not an easy decision. If you want a 'normal' job with a well-defined career path, it's easy to find career guidance. However, if you're a PACE person (as defined above), and want to do something a bit more unusual with your life, it's harder to find good advice. Here are a few notes just for you.

First of all, *it's totally okay* to have unusual ambitions. If you want to be an entertainer or do something creative and a bit unconventional, this is absolutely fine. I know plenty of PACE people: comedians, singers, magicians, jugglers, fire-eaters, a master puppeteer, a leading creature FX artist, a brilliant impressionist, several actors and a husband and wife team who do the world's best mindreading act. In short, if you can think of an unusual way to earn a living, I probably know someone who does it. If you feel like doing something similar, this book will help.

Don't *ignore* your parents, teachers and other people who want to help you. Listen to them and respect their experience. Just understand that they might not know much about strange, creative and unusual careers. Maybe you can discuss some sections of this book with them.

This book is not just about working for yourself. It's also about being able to pay your bills and support yourself. In other words, being a financially responsible adult.

Be under no illusions: working for yourself is *more* difficult than just doing a regular job in an office, shop or factory. Those of us who are drawn to the self-employed way of life *like* the fact that it is the harder option. It may be more challenging but it's also more fulfilling. Climbing the mountain is difficult but the view from the top is magnificent!

A Touch Of Magic

Some aspects of this book will make a bit more sense if I briefly explain a couple of points.

I'm basically a writer. I started off working in creative media and marketing before stumbling into the IT industry and becoming what is called a 'technical author'. I started working for myself in 1997, so I guess you could say I've been around a bit. Writing is still my main focus. I write and publish books for myself (like this one) and also 'ghost' books for other people.

I also run a few websites, do some corporate talks and training, mentor my private clients, occasionally run public classes and help people to start working for themselves.

I am not a professional magician. However, I am a keen amateur and magic is a large part of my life. I'm a member of the Magic Circle in London and have performed magic and mindreading shows all over the world. Via this minor involvement in the world of showbusiness and entertainment, I have met countless other performers and people with a dazzling array of strange talents. This is why this book contains several references to people who do strange things for a living.

* * *

What's Next?

If you're drawn towards working for yourself, you're not alone. In fact, there are soon going to be lots of people who see this as their only option. Why? Because we live in the age of magic technology, which means fewer normal jobs to go round. The next (very short) chapter provides a few more details about this.

2. Changing World, Fewer Jobs

"Let us remember: one book, one pen, one child, and one teacher can change the world."

— Malala Yousafzai

2. Changing World, Fewer Jobs

Here's the standard deal that society offers to most people:

> 1. During the week, work hard at a job you don't like very much. This usually means spending about forty hours a week in an office, shop or factory. You have to do this for all the best hours of the best years of your life.

> 2. In the evenings and at weekends, be an obedient, passive consumer. Buy lots of stuff and always want more. For your leisure and entertainment, watch other people do interesting things and pay for the privilege of doing so.

Self-employed people don't *despise* this deal. We know it suits some people. We just prefer a different journey. We don't care to do a job designed by someone else. We want to do a job we've devised for ourselves. Rather than switch on TV and watch someone else have an interesting career, we'd rather do interesting things ourselves.

The problem with this 'standard deal' is not just that it doesn't suit everyone. For many people, it's simply not going to be an option for much longer. We live in the age of magic technology. Computerisation, automation, artificial intelligence and robotics, plus the shift towards the online economy, have transformed the world of work.

Once upon a time, a new factory needed five hundred workers or more. Now it needs fifty and next year it may only need ten. At one point, to sell clothes you needed a chain of shops and a small army of staff. Now you need a good website and a few people in a warehouse. It's the same pattern wherever you look: companies need fewer people these days.

At the same time, the population of most countries is increasing. Result: more people chasing fewer jobs. What's more, the jobs don't pay as well as they used to in real terms. Wages haven't kept up with the cost of living for decades.

This book is not about politics. Regardless of your political affiliations, you've never seen a politician who could make time run backwards. The rise of magic technology means more people chasing fewer conventional jobs. The people without jobs can either live off social welfare payments or work for themselves. If they work for themselves but don't make much money, they'll still rely on the public purse.

Conclusion: we need to help more people to successfully work for themselves. I hope this book can be part of the solution.

Stats And Facts

It's true that you can make statistics tell any story you want. Nonetheless, a brief dabble in the murky waters of stats won't do us any harm.

The International Labour Organisation produced a report called 'World Employment Social Outlook / Trends 2016'. As you can probably guess, it's not exactly cheerful reading:

> "Decent work gaps remain pervasive across all regions in one form or another, from high rates of unemployment in developed economies to chronic vulnerable employment rates in many emerging and developing economies ... globally, there are over 2 billion working-age people who are not participating in the labour market. Some 26 million joined these ranks in 2015. According to ILO projections, participation rates are expected to stabilize at 62.8 per cent of the global working-age population."

In other words, more than a third of the working-age population don't have a job. What's more, nobody expects this situation is ever going to improve.

You and I can look at this data and turn the page. The ILO people, on the other hand, have to study these depressing figures all day, every day. I bet they have really cheerful office parties.

In 2013, the Oxford Martin School at the University of Oxford published 'The Future of Employment: How susceptible are jobs to computerisation?'. They concluded: "...about 47 per cent of total US employment is at risk (from computerisation)." In simple terms, about half the workforce could get replaced by a computer before too long. It's bad enough when you lose your job to another person. Think how you'll feel if you get replaced by a smirking box of silicon and metal.

You can find similar clouds of gloom wherever you care to look. The World Economic Forum website features a report on 'Employment Trends', focusing on the period 2015-2020. It says:

> "Without urgent and targeted action today to manage the near-term transition and build a workforce with future-proof skills, governments will have to cope with ever-growing unemployment and inequality."

In short, the free market economy can't deliver what it used to. This is why it's increasingly important for people to know how to work for themselves and earn a living.

The Price We All Pay

When people do unfulfilled jobs or lead unfulfilled lives, the social cost is enormous. Collectively, we all pay a very high price.

For example, some young people grow up feeling they have no hope of any kind of fulfilment. This often leads to delinquency and vandalism. It can even lead to violence and a drift towards extremist groups and beliefs. Think about the cost in terms of policing, social services and health care.

There's also the intangible cost of feeling less safe walking the streets, or seeing graffiti and vandalism everywhere. The International Labour Organisation 'WESO' report, which I mentioned earlier, has a delightfully cheery section on 'Intensified Risks of Social Unrest'. It says:

> "As growth slows in emerging and developing economies,
> social unrest has been on the rise ... as the economic situation
> began to deteriorate once more, most notably in developing
> economies, social unrest became more apparent."

It's not just younger people we have to think about. Middle-aged people can also fall prey to feelings of despair and lack of fulfilment. When they do, they often resort to various kinds of pseudo-fulfilment such as drinking and gambling. Alcohol abuse alone leads to many cases of violence and damage to property that we all end up paying for, one way or another.

For all of these reasons and more, I believe anything that helps people to lead more fulfilled lives creates a better society for us all. If this book can help at least a few people to do this, it will have been worthwhile.

* * *

What's Next?

It's clear a lot of people are going to be interested in working for themselves — either because they want to or they feel they have little alternative. So, if you want to work for yourself, how do you go about it? Well, your first priority is... you!

3. Get Yourself Ready

"A year from now you will wish you had started today."

— Karen Lamb

3. Get Yourself Ready

Here's your basic action plan for starting to work for yourself:

- Get yourself ready.

- Get your business set up.

- Get your product or service right.

- Start shouting about it (promotion).

This chapter, and the three that follow, will address each of these in turn. So, first of all, you need to get yourself ready for the wonderful world of self-employment.

Expectations And Attitude

Before you do anything else, open your eyes and have a good long think about whether you really want to do this. Here's the deal with self-employment: it's massively more difficult than working for someone else but also massively more rewarding and fulfilling. You need to be well aware of both halves of this picture.

When people tell me they are thinking of working for themselves, I like to be supportive and encouraging. However, there's no point in just offering a bright smile and saying, "Hey, go for it! You can do this!"

Here's the reality check. You're either cut out for this or you're not. When you work for someone else, you basically have one job to do. Anything else is someone else's problem. Computer glitches? Sales difficulties? Accounts issues? Not your concern — let someone else take the strain. When you work for yourself, every day is a problem day and every problem is *your* problem. If it's something you can deal with, it still takes time and effort. If not, you have to find someone who can.

You will have to make sacrifices and sometimes work very long hours to get everything done. There will be setbacks, problems and some steep learning curves. I'm not saying any of this to deter you. The points is that choosing to work for yourself is like any other journey: it helps if you have your eyes open before you set off.

So, do you feel sure this path is right for you? Sure, it's easy to want the highs, the rewards, the fulfilment and the success. But do you want them enough to put up with all the baggage that comes with them?

Health And Fitness

If you work for yourself, you're going to be working long hours, dealing with some stressful situations and using a lot of energy. There's a fairly obvious message here: the healthier you are, the more easily you'll cope with it all and the more you'll be able to get done.

A complete guide to mental, emotional and physical health is beyond the scope of this book. However, here's some good advice. First of all, starting paying attention to your MEDS:

- Meditation.

- Exercise.

- Diet.

- Sleep.

These are the cornerstones of health in both mind and body. I suggest you devote some time to learning about each of these areas. For example, you can learn how to meditate in half an hour by watching free online tutorials and YouTube videos. Always get enough sleep, by which I mean as much as your mind and body need to feel good. (If you happen to have babies or young children around, you will have quite rightly dismissed this suggestion with a hollow laugh and a snort of derision. I understand.)

You can learn about exercise and diet from books, trainers, videos or local classes. Alternatively, you can go to my Addiction Fixer website and get my book, 'The Easy-ish Way To Lose Weight And Get Fit'. Brief story: I was obese for about thirty years because I was addicted to sugar and starchy foods. I fought hard to overcome the addiction but always failed. Then, at long last, I discovered how to rid myself of the problem for good. I was able to lose a lot of weight (40 kilos or 88 lbs) and get myself fit enough to run 10 kilometres. You can do it too, as I explain in the book. No willpower or diets, no need to go to the gym or ever feel hungry. End of product promotion.

Think about any aspect of working for yourself and I can confidently make this promise: the healthier you are, in mind and body, the easier your journey is going to be. There are no guarantees when it comes to health because life isn't fair and illness can strike at random. However, when you pay attention to your MEDS (as defined above), you give yourself the best possible chance of staying healthy in mind and body. If you want to work for yourself and be successful, this is a really good way to play the odds.

Attitude

Here are some good attitudes to have:

- Love yourself and your potential.

- Love other people and the potential you see in them.

- Love life and its potential.

The part about 'loving other people' can be challenging. As you are probably well aware, there are times in life when other people can drive you crazy. Sartre said, "Hell is other people." Nonetheless, learning to love, respect and appreciate other people is important. Let me mention two points in particular.

First of all, *never* denigrate another human being. Always treat everyone with respect, politeness and kindness. You don't have to respect the other person's *ideas*. It's a good policy to only respect ideas that deserve to be respected. However, you should always respect the *person*.

Secondly, understand this: everyone is doing the best they can with what they have. When you're born, you get dealt a hand of cards. You spend the rest of your life playing those cards as best you can, trying to achieve security, fulfilment, pleasure and contentment. This is what we are all doing, every day. The people who you think have treated you badly? They're just doing the best they can with what they have. Same as you, same as me, same as everyone else. Understand this and engrave it on your mind and your heart. This isn't easy to do but it's a good idea all the same.

Invest In Yourself

When you work for yourself, you're going to earn money based on what you know and what you can do. It's a good idea to make progress in both these areas as often as you can. Always strive to broaden your skill based, get more qualifications and climb a few more learning curves. This won't always be easy but it's always worth doing.

It's better to grow than to stagnate. Also, acquiring new knowledge and skills, while it can be time-consuming and challenging, is also usually a lot of fun if you approach it in the right spirit. It's nice to go from "I can't" to "I can".

The more you know and can do, the more *value* you can offer the world. The more value you can offer, the more *money* you can earn.

Fall In Love With Commercial Reality

People who are considering self-employment often think about all the good things it could lead to: doing something you enjoy, financial success, loyal customers and so on. However, none of these things are where you *start* from. These are all things that may come later, towards the *end* of your journey. You start by falling in love with commercial reality. Here are the basics:

1. You provide value, you get money. No value? No money. More value? More money.

2. It is not the market's job to find you. It is your job to find (or create) a market for your work.

3. It is not the market's job to please you. It is your job to please the market.

4. Doing some productive work, and making a bit of money, is far more enjoyable than wondering why the world isn't solving your problems for you.

Don't feel daunted or dismayed by commercial reality. Feel enthused and inspired by it. See it as a magical key to success. Realise that *every* time you offer value, you can make money. What's more, you can try as many ideas as you want, as often as you want.

Commercial reality is not a problem, a bind, a chain around your spirit. It is your magic carpet to success and fulfilment.

Nobody Starts At The Top

One aspect of falling in love with commercial reality is this: recognise that you don't get to start at the top. It would be nice if you could but unfortunately life just doesn't work that way. The bright days of sweet success and great rewards come along *eventually,* if you work for them. However, they are not where you *start.*

Every ladder works the same way: you start at the bottom and climb up. Acknowledging this can involve a little bit of humility. At one time, back in the 'swing' era, Frank Sinatra was just an unknown young singer trying to get some work. He went to clubs where dance bands and orchestras were unloading their stuff and offered to help carry it in. In return, he asked them to let him sing a couple of songs. That's how he got started. Follow his example. Swallow your pride and do what you have to do.

The Unhappy Artist

I was once chatting with an artist friend of mine. She wasn't very happy because she hardly ever had any money. "Everyone wants art," she said, in a rather dejected tone, "but nobody wants to pay for it."

She was talented and willing to work hard. However, she hadn't learned to accept commercial reality. In effect, she was complaining because the market wasn't pleasing her. Well, this isn't the market's job. If she wanted to make money, it was her responsibility to please the market.

Her experience was good information that she *could* have acted on in a positive way. If she had tried to earn money in one way, and found it didn't work, she could have learned from this experience and looked for something else that *would* work. A self-pity session was pointless and an insult to her own potential. Trying out her next idea, with a cheerful, positive spirit, would have been a much better step.

Entertainer Economics

Are you what I have described as a PACE person? Do you want to be a performer or an entertainer? Great! It's a wonderful vocation and the world needs good entertainment.

A friend of mine called Neil is a singer who also does a bit of comedy between songs. He went to a local pub that had a small performance area. He said to the owner, "If you let me use that space for free on one of your quiet nights, I'll put on a weekly show of music and comedy with a few other performers I know. We'll see to all the promotion. We'll get all our friends to come and they'll buy lots of drinks so you'll make more money than you normally would." The owner agreed and allowed Neil to use the space. He promoted the weekly show and divided the revenue from tickets between himself and other performers who took part.

Was any of this easy? No. Promoting the shows and running them well took a lot of time, effort and energy. There were often problems to deal with and some weeks, despite Neil's promotional efforts, the size of the audience was rather disappointing. Nonetheless, running these weekly shows was a fantastic learning experience and, more often than not, pretty good fun into the bargain. It was also a way for Neil to make some money every week doing something he enjoyed, some of which he could re-invest in his career.

You can study economics and business development books for years if you want to. Alternatively, you can just remember this story about Neil because it's pretty much all you need to know.

My First Job

My first job was with a creative media and marketing company. They had facilities for graphic design, 24-track sound recording and video production. The owner got lots of letters from young people who wanted to work there. They often said things like, "Please give me a job — I'll do anything you want. I'll even make the coffee."

As my boss pointed out, the people who wrote these letters were demonstrating that they didn't understand *anything* about commercial reality and were therefore unemployable. He could make his own coffee and, in any case, having someone to make coffee wouldn't bring in any money. He never even replied to any of these letters.

I got a job at this place for one reason: they needed someone to research and write scripts and they thought I was fairly good at it. Of course, I had to prove myself. I went to see them (with my portable typewriter) and they briefed me on a video they were working on. They put me up in a hotel overnight and asked to have a go at writing the script for the video. When I went back in the morning, with my script ready, they read it and, luckily, felt it was good enough to make me a job offer.

They didn't give me a job because they liked the look of my face or felt like giving me a chance. They did it because it made commercial sense. I was able to do some work that added to the company's profits. They were happy to pay me X because the work I did generated more than X for the company.

These days I run my own business but the commercial realities haven't changed. The reason people hire me to do this or that is because I deliver value that they figure is worth the money. It's that simple.

The fundamental laws of economic exchange are the same for us all. If you can deliver value, you can make money. No value, no money. More value, more money.

* * *

What's Next?

The next step is to actually set up your business. This is the the subject of the next section, which also includes several things you should be careful *not* to do.

4. Get Your Business Set Up

"If you want to make your dreams come true, the first thing you have to do is wake up."

— J. M. Power

4. Get Your Business Set Up

Here's a reminder of the four sections we're working through:

- Get yourself ready.

- Get your business set up.

- Get your product or service right.

- Start shouting about it (promotion).

The last section was about getting yourself ready, so now let's move on to getting your business ready.

Find Your Mentor

First, find your Mentor. This means someone who seems relatively successful, has a positive attitude and can offer relevant experience.

Whether you want to be a session musician, get into stand-up comedy, perform a balancing act in a circus, be a tree surgeon or set up a catering business, find someone who is already doing it and who seems fairly happy with their situation. If you can find your mentor in real life, great. If not, find one online.

Explain your plans and intentions and ask you mentor if they would agree to have a chat from time to time and answer a few questions. If they're happy to do this for free, great. If not, discuss payment options and see if you can come to an agreement. If you can't, you'll just have to find someone else.

If your mentor doesn't ask for payment, get creative and find a way to offer them some value in return for their occasional input and advice. Aim to be a giver first and a taker second. Don't go through life expecting something for nothing.

You might wonder why anyone would agree to be your mentor if you are, in effect, going to be in competition with them? Well, a few people might refuse to be your mentor for precisely this reason. However, most potential mentors won't worry about this. For one thing, anyone who is good at what they do isn't worried about competition. There's always enough work to go round for people who offer value. Secondly, they are way ahead of you. If you somehow manage to catch up and overtake them, whose fault is that?

28

See To The Legal And Accounting Stuff

Next, see to the boring legal and accounting stuff.

When you work for yourself, there are a few different options available to you. These will vary according to the laws and regulations where you happen to live. In the UK, where I'm based, most self-employed people choose to be either what's called a 'sole trader' or a 'private limited company'. In the United States, I'm told there are options such as Sole Proprietorship, Limited Liability Company, type 'C' Corporation or a sub-chapter 'S' Corporation.

If you don't understand the difference between these various options, don't worry. Nobody does when they're starting out. Ask your mentor about your options or go to see an accountant or legal advisor. Say:

> "I'm thinking of working for myself. Please tell me the basics of what I need to know, including whether I should be a 'sole trader' or a 'limited company' or something else. What are the pros and cons of each option? Also, please tell me what records I need to keep, whether I need to set up a separate bank account and how taxation works."

If you go to see an accountant, this initial consultation is usually free (or at least very inexpensive) because they hope you'll become a client. Then again, you might decide not to have an accountant and do your own taxes at the end of the year, if this is an option where you live. Your local authority might also have useful resources, including some free advice and explanatory literature. Likewise, the tax authorities in your country will have a website full of free information.

You will usually, though not always, need to set up a separate bank account for all your trade or business transactions. If so, choose a bank and ask them how much it costs to have a business account and how their scale of charges works. Shop around to get the best deal.

Attend to any other legalities that are involved in the kind of business you want to run. For example, if you are making and selling anything edible, you will have to comply with regulations about hygiene and the safe preparation of food. Again, the best sources of guidance are (a) the officials in your area whose job it is to give out this sort of information, and (b) your mentor.

Don't ignore all this legal and accounting stuff even if you find it mind-numbingly boring (as many self-employed people do). Make sure that in legal terms your business is squeaky clean, well advised and ready to go. It doesn't have to take long.

Understand The Financial Basics

To run your own successful business, you don't have to be a financial genius. However, there are a few things you *do* need to understand, starting with tax.

When you have a regular job, your employer pays you each week or month but (in most cases) they deduct the appropriate income tax before they pay you. Your *gross* wage or salary is the amount before tax is taken out. The amount left over, that you actually receive, is your *net* pay. You are free to use your net pay however you want because the tax has already been taken out.

When you work for yourself, there isn't anyone automatically calculating how much tax you owe the government and deducting it each week or each month. The money you get paid for doing whatever you do is your *gross* income. At some point in the financial year, you have to do some calculations and hand over a chunk of tax. What's left over is your *net* pay, to use as you wish.

Some people calculate their own taxes and deal directly with the tax authorities. Others get an accountant or financially qualified person to do it all for them (which costs money, of course).

Many businesses hardly ever involve cash payments. For example, you do some work for a customer and send them an invoice (a request to be paid for what you did). They pay you via online banking. This means there are records of the transaction at both ends. If anyone from the tax office wanted to check up on you, they could see two records: the money going *out* of the customer's account and the corresponding amount going *in* to your account.

What if you get paid in cash? As there's no record of the transaction, you might think you could simply not declare this income (not tell the tax authorities about it) and keep it all for yourself. This is known as doing business 'off the books'. Please don't be tempted to do this.

For one thing, it's immoral and greedy. Taxation pays for the services we all, collectively, rely on so we should all pay our share. Secondly, it's illegal and sooner or later you *will* get caught. Once you've been caught, you won't like the punishment. What's more, from that point on the tax authorities can make life very difficult for you, for example by running audits and requesting extra paperwork. The best advice is this: be really *boring* as far as the authorities are concerned and never give them a reason to find you interesting or worth investigating. Keep everything you do legal, pay your taxes and don't have anything to hide. It's the right thing to do and you'll also sleep more easily at night.

Some Financial Terminology

So far, so good. You understand the difference between gross and net income and you're going to play by the rules and pay all your taxes. There's not much else for you to understand but let's just skim over a few other bits of business jargon and terminology.

Your *turnover* is how much your customers pay you over a given amount of time, say in a given quarter (three month period) or year. Not all of this money is *profit*, because running any business involves some operating costs. For example, you may have to pay for some raw materials or to hire equipment.

Your revenue minus your costs is your *gross profit*. You have to pay an amount of tax on this. Once the tax people have taken their bite, what's left is your *net profit*. This is what really matters to you because it tells you how much you've got left over, which you can either save or spend on stuff you want/need.

If you have formed a company or corporation, there will be two sets of tax calculations: one for your company and another for you as an individual. Your company has to pay corporation tax on its gross profits. When your company pays some money to you, as an individual, you have to pay income tax on your gross income just as you would if you had a normal job. Your company pays corporation tax. You pay your personal income tax.

The jargon and terminology may be different in your part of the world. Every country seems to have its own jargon and way of describing the same basic ideas. Nonetheless, the basic concepts will be the same no matter which country you live in.

There's a saying in business: 'turnover is vanity, profit is sanity'. If you have high turnover, meaning that a lot of money is coming in to your company, you might feel rather pleased and excited. Look at all this money raining down from the sky! I'm doing really well!

However, your turnover on its own doesn't tell you much. You have your operating costs and tax to consider. What you're left with after costs and tax is your (net) profit, and that's the real indication of how well you're doing. It's possible to have very high turnover but very low profits.

If you want to develop a more detailed understanding of financial stuff, educate yourself about it, consult a professional or have a chat with your mentor.

Let's move on to other aspects of getting your business ready.

Your Business Plan

You've found your mentor, seen to all the legal and accounting stuff and you understand basic financial jargon.

The next step is to prepare your business plan. This means estimating how many customers you'll get per month, your approximate revenue, your costs and therefore your profit. Keep all your estimates conservative and realistic (in other words, avoid wildly optimistic expectations).

Some people prepare very thorough and detailed business plans while others hardly prepare one at all. As with so much in life, the smart move is to avoid the extremes. Don't get so obsessed with planning that you never actually start your business. If six months have gone by and you are still devising plans, something's wrong. On the other hand, not doing any sort of planning at all is a poor strategy. As motivational speakers like to say, "If you fail to plan, you plan to fail." Have at least a basic plan in mind and revise it in the light of experience.

Practicalities

Next, see to the practicalities: Premises, Equipment, Suppliers.

Where will your business be based? Most people who start working for themselves simply choose to work from home. This is the easiest and least expensive option. However, if you need separate premises (for example to set up a workshop) you'll need to find a suitable place, get it suitably fitted out and make it ready for business.

What equipment do you need? Also, do you need any specific supplies, such as materials and components? If so, you'll need to track down appropriate suppliers.

When you're seeing to all these practicalities, there are two golden rules:

1. Start small, simple and humble.

2. Spend as little as possible.

When you start a business, the aim is to *make* money rather than spend it. Every penny you spend is more money you need to make back before you move into profit. So, when you start, become Super Scrooge. Don't spend one cent that isn't absolutely essential. When you've made a small but healthy profit, you can invest some of it in the business and buy better equipment or nicer tools. But when you start, spend as close to zero as possible.

Don't Get Stuck On Trivia

When you set up your new business or venture, your top priority should be simple: get to the stage where you have some money coming in.

To this end, I suggest you don't get hung up on trivial details. Don't spend months just trying to settle on a name for your business or getting a logo designed. You're wasting time. If your name is Jill Smith, start trading as Jill Smith or, if you form a company, Jill Smith Limited (or however companies are designated in your country). If you think of a tremendously witty name for your business later on, you can change it. It's not something you need to think about in the early stages.

Your website domain can be jillsmith.com or, if this has been taken, the simplest and closest equivalent you can get.

You don't need a logo when you're launching your business. If you must have one, keep it simple. Choose a geometrical shape (square, circle, hexagon or whatever) and make this any colour you like. Put your initials inside it using a nice font and a different colour that goes well with the first one. That's your logo, done! It probably won't win the 'Company Logo Of The Year' award but it will do for the time being. If you spend more than fifteen minutes on this, you're wasting your time.

Need some letterhead paper and business cards? Go into any high street print shop, give them your details, choose a 'stock' design and they'll get it done in a day or two.

Need a website? To begin with, all you need is a simple 'display' website that says who you are, what you do and how to contact you. There are lots of ways to set up a simple website quickly. Just Google 'create simple website' and see what you find. If necessary, get a friend who's good at writing to add a little sales 'dazzle' (or hire me to do it for you). Other self-employed people will help you to get all this done.

Start small, simple and humble. Focus on what you can do, make or sell that people will pay for and *get some money coming in*.

Just to be clear, 'start simple' doesn't mean 'look cheap'. For example, if you have any money at all, and if you're going to use business cards, it's worth investing in ones that are fairly good quality. Cheap, badly printed cards on thin stock make a poor first impression and suggest you don't think much of yourself.

You may also want to look at my booklet, 'A Simple Introduction To Marketing'. You can download this instantly, completely free of charge, from www.ianrowland.com .

Don't Chase Grants

If you want to set up a new business, there may be some grants and subsidies available to you. Over the years, I've seen people who seem to spend 10% of their time running their business and 90% filling in forms to apply for grants. They usually say, "Why turn down free money if it's there just waiting to be claimed?"

Well, I can think of a few reasons:

1. There's a lot of paperwork involved. I didn't choose to work for myself because I want to spend my life filling in forms and dealing with bureaucrats.

2. There are always strings attached. If someone's offering a grant, there will be terms and conditions involved, some of which you might not like.

3. The tap can be turned off at any moment. You never know when a particular scheme will be cut back or cancelled. It's easy to become so reliant on lazy money that when the grant is withdrawn, your business collapses.

Aim for *customers,* not grants. Aim for *profits,* not subsidies. The reality is that there's either a market for your work or there isn't. If there is, you don't need grants and subsidies. If there isn't, then the grants are just masking the truth and one day they'll run out.

Don't Start Off In A Partnership

When starting your business, I strongly advise you not to do so in partnership with someone else. Why not? Because one person *always* ends up putting in more effort than the other, doing more of the hard work and being responsible for more of the income. This leads to friction and disagreement.

Yes, there are exceptions because there are exceptions to everything. It worked out well for Mr. Rolls and Mr. Royce. Likewise for Mr. Cocac and Mr. Ola, who created the world's most popular fizzy drink. However, these happy marriages are extremely rare. In the early days of your career, I suggest you fly solo.

By all means *collaborate* with other self-employed people and work together on specific projects. This can be great fun and highly productive. Just don't create your business as a partnership. Work for yourself and maintain control of your business destiny.

34

Don't Think Buying Is Achieving

Anyone can buy an expensive camera. Owning the camera doesn't get anything done. You have to learn how to use it in a skilful way to produce interesting and beautiful shots. This is work. It's the work that achieves something, not the owning.

You might think this is an obvious distinction and I agree that it *ought* to be. Unfortunately, many people have a serious work avoidance problem. They're good at buying stuff but seem highly reluctant to ever actually do any work.

Saying is not doing. Buying is not achieving. When you put in some work and achieve something, that's when people will take you seriously, including other self-employed people. It's also when you might start to actually make some money.

Don't Believe Most Ventures Fail

If you read one or two books about working for yourself, you might well come across the idea that 95% of new businesses fail in their first year. The percentage quoted may vary, but this gloomy message crops up a lot in books and leaflets about working for yourself. Anyone who recites this nonsense doesn't know what they're talking about. Let me give you a slightly more accurate version.

95% of businesses started by reckless people with little value to offer, who spend a lot money without any realistic prospect of ever making a profit, go out of business within their first year and deserve to.

Conversely, 95% of businesses started by thoughtful people, who understand commercial reality, who have a product for which there is some demand, who work hard and take care to spend as little money as possible at first, and who remember to start small, simple and humble, will almost certainly survive for years.

Don't Worry About Constraints

During the early days of being self-employed, you will probably have fairly limited resources. This is normal.

Maybe you'd like to rent an office and hire a secretary but you can't afford to do so and therefore just work from home instead. Maybe you're a musician and want to buy the latest digital recorder but it's beyond your means. Perhaps you'd like to be making your product in a purpose-built workshop but you can't, so you have to use your basement, garage, kitchen or yard. This is what the early days of most new businesses are like.

Don't worry about what you *don't* have or *can't* do. It's a waste of your time, energy and emotion. Just focus on what you *do* have and what you *can* do.

It's a good idea to appreciate that sometimes, limitations and constraints are spurs to creative thinking. Someone once said that creative work is like a diamond: it is formed under pressure.

Movie director Robert Rodriguez was once lecturing to some film students. These students were always hearing about big Hollywood movies with budgets running into tens or hundreds of millions of dollars, while they themselves barely had any money at all for their projects. Rodriguez advised them not to worry about this. He said, "Always remember that you can do something the Hollywood executives don't know how to do. All of you know how to make a movie for $5000 and finish it in three months. Nobody in Hollywood knows how to do that."

Rodriguez was making a very good point. In 1992, he had a big hit with a movie called 'El Mariachi', which he wrote and directed. When he made this film, Rodriguez had very limited resources. In fact the total budget is said to have been just $7000. As Rodriguez mentioned in interviews, this tiny budget forced him to be creative, to figure out how to make his movie despite having hardly anything to make it with. ('El Mariachi' went on to make $2 million at the box office.)

Don't worry about constraints. Work *with* them. They force you to be creative.

* * *

What's Next?

You won't have much of a business if you don't have a product or service to sell. In the next section, we'll look at getting your product right, which includes something called the PIO Principle.

5. Get Your Product Right

"Talent is cheaper than table salt. What separates the talented individual from the successful one is a lot of hard work."

— Stephen King

5. Get Your Product Right

Here are the four sections we're working through:

- Get yourself ready.

- Get your business set up.

- Get your product or service right.

- Start shouting about it (promotion).

Let's look at getting your product or service right.

Deciding What To Sell

If you already know what your product or service is going to be, you can skip to the next section, 'The Product Reality Check'.

If not, here are a few ways of thinking about products and services you could sell. They may spur some ideas or help you to bring your own thoughts into focus.

Need / Want / Aspiration

A product is anything people are willing to pay for. Some traditional marketing textbooks divide products into groups, depending on whether they meet a need, a want or an aspiration.

A **need**: something people buy not because they particularly *want* to, but just because it meets a basic need. Example: a toothbrush.

A **want**: something people don't actually *need* but buy for reasons such as convenience, pleasure, leisure and fun. Example: a child wanting a bicycle. It is *possible* to live without a bicycle but nonetheless a child may want one with a desire that burns like the mid-day sun in Rio.

An **aspiration**: items bought by people who think buying something expensive confers 'status' and is a substitute for having a life. Example: a watch that costs over £20,000. What does it do? It tells the time.

If you're wondering what you could sell, this way of assessing products may help you to come up with some ideas. Which needs, wants or aspirations could you satisfy in a profitable way?

Selling Propositions

Another way to think about products you could offer is to consider what are known as 'selling propositions'. A selling proposition just means a basic reason why someone might want to buy something. There are many selling propositions but here are five very common ones:

- I can fulfil a need you have.

- I can give you something you want (at a good price).

- I can solve your problem.

- I can save you money.

- I can offer an enjoyable experience.

Think about the different kinds of work that people do and the various selling propositions involved. Take a look at the stores and businesses in your neighbourhood and think about the various selling propositions involved. This might give you ideas about how to make money from your own skills, talents, knowledge and willingness to provide value.

The PIO Principle

Another good way to think about products is simply this: products exist to solve problems.

If we all lived in a perfect world of peaches and paradise, where everyone had everything they wanted all the time, nobody would ever create any new products or services. There would be no need. Luckily for anyone interested in starting a business, this is not the case.

Since products exist to solve problems, it follows that *problems indicate opportunities*. I call this the PIO principle.

If you encounter an annoying problem, see it as an opportunity to create something. Ask yourself if lots of other people might be experiencing the same problem. If so, maybe you can develop a product or service that solves the problem or makes it more tolerable.

Don't just pay attention to your own annoyances and problems. Listen to other people too. If you hear several people having a good moan about the same thing, this indicates an opportunity to create something that takes the problem away. Always remember: problems indicate opportunities (PIO).

What Value Can You Offer?

Here's another way to spur a few thoughts about the product or service you could offer to the world.

There's only one reason why anyone ever buys anything: because they perceive some value in whatever goods or services are involved. Think about this. What value do you want to give to other people?

Do you want to create a great product? Do you want to share your specific knowledge, expertise or insight? Do you want to create art or entertain people? If you look deep down inside yourself, what is it you really want to do with your time, energy, experience and talents? What goal, dream or ambition would inspire you to work long hours and make a few sacrifices?

Taking the short-term view, what value can you give right now to other people, or to companies and organisations? How can you make their life better, easier or more enjoyable? What problems can you solve for them in a way that they'll be willing to pay for?

Taking the long-term view, many years from now when you approach the final chapters of your story, what do you want to look back on with pride and satisfaction? What role do you want to have played? What contribution do you want to have made?

Find The Golden Eagle In You

If you see a golden eagle gliding majestically across the skies, effortlessly riding thermal currents while spotting prey on the distant horizon, you may think it looks rather magnificent. However, the eagle isn't aware that it is doing anything particularly impressive because it's just doing what comes naturally. (I watched the eagles when I trekked through parts of the Mojave desert and they are truly *magnificent* creatures.)

In a similar way, many people have strengths and talents they aren't aware of because they just come naturally or feel effortless. If you're trying to figure out what value you can offer, talk to people who know you well and who can help you to identify your strengths and potential. They may be able to see things about you that you can't see for yourself.

However, the people you talk to have to be completely honest with you. If they just say nice things to encourage you and be supportive, this won't tell you anything. Bear in mind that if you ask people to be totally honest, you have to be ready to hear honest views and opinions! If you don't want the truth, or can't handle it, then don't ask for it.

The Product Reality Check

Let's say you have an idea for a product or service you want to offer. I suggest you apply a reality check before you do anything else. The best way to do this is to consult people who have more relevant experience than you of your intended market. Find other self-employed people who will listen to your ideas and give you the benefit of their experience. If you can't find them in real life, find them online.

You won't always hear what you want to hear. People who work for themselves generally like to be supportive but they are also very practical — especially when it comes to financial survival. If several experienced, self-employed people tell you that your ideas probably won't make money, then it's time for a re-think.

A Useful Checklist

A product is only worthwhile if it will generate sufficient profit for you to enjoy a decent standard of living. Consider these questions.

1. Is there really a significant demand? What leads you to think that there is? Can you estimate or measure the extent of it? Have you done your research?

2. Who wants your product or service? Who is your 'target demographic' — the group of people you expect to pay you?

3. Is it realistic to think you can reach these people via promotion and advertising? Assuming you can, is it also likely that a sufficient percentage of them will be willing to pay your asking price?

4. What competition will you face? How will you be able to compete effectively? What can you offer that others can't? How can you differentiate yourself or your product and why are people likely to prefer it?

5. Even if all goes according to plan, will you generate sufficient profit to be able to support yourself and pay all your bills? Taking all your costs into consideration, is your profit margin going to be sufficient to give you a viable business?

6. Will your business be sustainable? Assuming you manage to get some initial sales, what's likely to happen after that? Will you get a steady stream of customers for the foreseeable future or will your sales, and revenue, dry up fairly quickly?

You won't be able to answer these questions with certainty. The point is to make the best and most realistic estimates you can. If you're too optimistic, you won't do yourself any favours. You could find yourself trying to sell something that isn't wanted, or at least isn't wanted enough to yield the level of profit you want. Being too pessimistic is no good either. You could talk yourself out of an idea that would, in fact, produce a perfectly viable and healthy business.

You just have to be as honest and realistic as you can, do your research and take advice from people with relevant experience.

Multiple Products

Throughout this book, I usually refer to self-employed people as having one product rather than several. This is partly for simplicity and partly because most people do, in fact, tend to have just one product — at least when they are starting out.

Of course, some self-employed people have more than one string to their bow. My favourite example is someone whose business card said, 'Face painter, Tarot reader, Chiropractor'. How's that for versatility?

If you can successfully offer a range of products or services, giving each the time and attention it deserves, then good for you. However, there are some dangers to be aware of. One is that you might spread your time and talent too thinly to be effective or successful. The other is that people who are in a position to give you work might not feel they have a clear idea of what you do. I cover this point in more detail later, in a section called 'The Madonna Gardening Book Theory'.

One Talent, Many Opportunities

If your product is a particular talent you have or a specific area of expertise, try to think about all the different markets in which it might have some value. One talent can mean many opportunities.

My friend Federica speaks four languages. When she began working for herself, she had no idea how to exploit her talent. In time, she discovered that she can use her skills in so many different ways it's hard to count them.

She helps companies to conduct foreign visitors around factories, and translates advertising literature. Some days she does bus tour commentaries for tourists, other days she assists with multi-lingual online conferences. She does some personal teaching and helps musicians translate songs and scores. She also works for companies that prepare educational and technical training courses, helping them to adapt their work to suit different global territories. One talent, many opportunities.

I have another friend, Marika, who is a very talented singer. She couldn't care less about the charts and has never had a hit single or wanted to. She's great fun to know and far more interesting than any pop singer I've ever seen being interviewed on TV. Guess what? She has a fantastic, fulfilled life as a singer.

She sings in shows, sings at all kinds of private events and parties all over Europe, runs a choir or two, does bits of media work, gives singing lessons and also teaches executives how to develop their presence, power and influence by using their voice correctly. She's been doing this successfully for years. It's a better path than someone who has a short-lived pop career, consisting of a couple of hit singles, and then wonders what to do with the rest of their life.

The more you think about how to apply your skill, talent, knowledge, training and expertise to other contexts, the more good ideas you'll come up with.

* * *

What's Next?

You've got yourself, your company and your product ready. Well done! The next state isn't hard to guess. You need to find yourself some customers. How do you go about this? Simple... you shout a lot!

6. Shout About It

"He was a dreamer, a thinker, a speculative philosopher. Or, as his wife would have it, an idiot."

— Douglas Adams

6. Shout About It

We have so far worked through three of these four sections:

- Get yourself ready.

- Get your business set up.

- Get your product or service right.

- Start shouting about it (promotion).

As you can see, the fourth and final part of launching your business is to shout about it. This is more formally known as promotion.

Marketing Basics

Marketing is the process of *optimising* your relationship with your market. For example, it may involve market research (finding out what your customers want) and product development (coming up with ideas your customers will like).

One part of marketing is promotion, and one subset of this is advertising. The short guide to promotion looks like this:

1. Decide on your key messages. What are the two or three short, key points you want to make about your product or service? How can you convey the appeal of your product in the simplest, clearest way? What simple, memorable promise do you want to make to the consumer?

2. You've decided on the key messages that are at the core of your promotion. Next, choose some 'marketing channels', ways to get your short, simple messages to your target market. Typical examples include: distributing leaflets, selling door-to-door, 'cold calling' on the phone, point-of-sale material, press advertising, broadcast or social media advertising, trade fairs, free public seminars, standing on the street holding a placard or shouting through a loudspeaker.

3. Decide how you're going to use the marketing channels you've chosen. What time and budget are you going to allocate to each one? Do you need to involve anyone else, such as getting a designer to create the leaflets you are going to distribute? Or can you do it all yourself?

Promotion Mythology

I don't know why, but business promotion seems to be one of those subjects that always attracts a lot of mythology and misinformation. I just want to make two things clear.

First of all, promotion is not magic. You can't take a product and, by some dazzling process of brilliant promotion, convince the whole world to buy it. Successful promotion is actually rather straightforward: do your research, gather data, refine your messages, choose your channels, use them well. It's important but not particularly exciting.

Secondly, all the promotion in the world can't make a bad product into a good one. If you don't have a good product, no amount of promotional effort can rescue it. The purpose of good promotion is to convey a message: here's something you might want and why you might want it. It is not to fool, deceive or trick customers into paying money for rubbish.

Quick Guide To Promotion

If you don't know a great deal about how to market, promote and sell your product, it won't take you long to learn. Here are the simplest and easiest steps I can recommend.

1. Read my short booklet called, 'A Simple Introduction To Marketing'. This won't cost you anything. It's a free, instant download you can get from www.ianrowland.com .

2. Read a book called 'Ogilvy on Advertising' by legendary advertising genius David Ogilvy. It's still the best book ever written on the subject and his sharp, incisive writing style is compelling.

3. Go online and search for 'The Theory And Practice Of Selling The Aga Cooker'. This was also written by David Ogilvy and you can read it free of charge. It's the perfect expression of how a top sales professional thinks about selling a product.

4. Read Brian Tracy, 'The Psychology of Selling', which is a concise, modern classic on the subject. Also, read any of the material put out by my friend Wes Schaeffer, The Sales Whisperer.

Then, stop reading, decide how you're going to shout about whatever you want to sell and do it!

Forms Of Promotion

People sometimes ask me which is the best way to promote their business. The answer is: whichever way gets best results. I know people who have started very successful businesses just by getting a few leaflets printed and pushing them through doors in their neighbourhood. Others allocate two hours every morning to 'cold calling' potential customers on the phone. Social media advertising can also be very effective if you know how to use it well or can find someone who does.

Don't be afraid to try more than one approach, and explore a range of marketing channels, in order to find out what generates the best results. Never make the mistake of believing you know everything about how to promote yourself. New opportunities come along all the time, as society and technology changes.

Finally, everyone who works for themselves will tell you the same thing: the greatest and most powerful form of advertising is simply WOM, which stands for 'word-of-mouth'.

You can't buy good WOM advertising but you can certainly encourage it. Provide a great product or service. Build good relationships with your customers, treat them as people (not just buyers) and keep them happy. Under-promise and over-deliver. Go the extra mile and never let a single customer down. Never leave a customer with a problem if you can leave them with a smile. Bad service is commonplace; good service with a helpful attitude and a smile gets noticed and goes a long way. (I'll say more about WOM in a later chapter called, 'About Making Money'.)

The Opposite Of Conceited

I sometimes work with private clients to help them grow their business. When I talk to them about promotion, they sometimes raise an interesting point. "I understand that I need to promote my business," they say, "but I don't want to come across as vain or conceited. I don't want to be the sort of person who is always telling everyone how great I am or what fantastic products I make."

This issue has interesting cultural roots. In some countries and cultures, it's perfectly acceptable to proclaim how brilliant you are. This is seen as admirable self-belief. In other cultures, it's far less acceptable.

I happen to live in England where the only socially acceptable attitude is to be self-deprecating and spend your entire life apologising for having the audacity to exist. Anyone promoting their work, or demonstrating any trace of positive self-esteem, is assumed to have mental health issues. By an act of law dating back to 1746, all such people are taken round the back of the Tower Of London and made to eat gravel until they admit the error of their ways. This time-honoured 'Gravel And Grovel' ceremony has become a popular tourist attraction. It can be enjoyed twice daily, at ten o'clock in the morning and three o'clock in the afternoon, except on Tuesdays.

Here's what I suggest to my private clients — especially the English ones with a morbid fear of self-promotion.

Yes, it's good to avoid being vain or conceited. However, there's no merit in being too self-deprecating either. There's nothing admirable about failing to provide the value you *could* give to people — whether this involves entertaining them, helping them to live a better life or supplying a product they'll appreciate.

If you're constantly talking about yourself and how great you are, you're conceited. If you're happy to talk about your success but also take an interest in other people and how great *they* are, and the value you see in them, this shows a more balanced and less self-centred attitude.

In other words, you avoid being conceited not by failing to believe in yourself but by believing in yourself *and* believing in other people as well. The way to fix "I'm great" is not to say "I'm not great". It's to say, "I'm great... and so are you."

Finally, I suggest you split your personal and professional lives to some extent. In your personal and private life, be as quiet and modest as you like. As regards your business, let your self-belief and self-confidence shine out of you like bright sunshine. Pursue every chance to tell your market what you do and why they want it. Shout, shout and shout again. If ever you feel uncomfortable doing this, trust me, you'll feel a lot more uncomfortable not being able to pay the rent or buy food!

* * *

What's Next?

To have a successful business, you don't just need a good product — you also need good productivity. This is what the next section is all about. We'll look at the difference between 'organise' and 'improvise' and find out what's meant by the 'internot'.

7. About Productivity

"I like work; it fascinates me. I can sit and look at it for hours."

— Jerome K. Jerome

7. About Productivity

When you work for yourself, you never feel you have enough time to do everything and always wish you could be more productive. In this chapter, I want to share some good ways to increase your productivity.

Organise, Don't Improvise

There are basically two ways to build your business.

One is to wake up each day and improvise, making it up as you go along and hoping you'll remember to get a few things done. The other is to organise how you spend your time. The difference between these two options is that one of them works.

An organised approach to your business, or indeed your life, is much better than cheerfully chaotic improvisation. I never see being organised as a chore. I see it as freedom. Being organised gives me clarity: I know exactly what I need to achieve each day. Organisation is also a great antidote to stress. It means I'm never worried about whether I've done the things I meant to do. Improvisation leads to stress just as organisation leads to peace.

You don't have to take this to extremes. I'm not suggesting you become a robotic organisation freak. I'm just saying that an organised approach to each day works better than making it up as you go along. If you're not a very organised person by nature, let me offer a few helpful suggestions.

Diary

Get a diary. It can take any form you like: a physical book, a document on your computer, a bit of software or whatever. In your diary, write down every commitment you make, every appointment, booking, gig or meeting. Refer to it daily and keep it up to date. As the Chinese proverb says, "The faintest ink is more powerful than the strongest memory." Write down anything you need to remember.

Incidentally, it's quite common (especially on the internet) to see little gems of wisdom described as a 'Chinese proverb' when they actually have nothing whatsoever to do with China. However, this line about ink and memory really is an old Chinese proverb! You can read about it online if you want to. Apparently it dates back to the Kangxi period of the Qing dynasty.

'To do' List

Make a 'To do' list. This can be a list written on a piece of paper, a simple text file or anything else that suits you. Refer to it every day and keep it updated.

When you think of something you want to get done, add it to the list. When you give someone a commitment that you'll do something, add it to the list.

Break down large goals into small, individual tasks. A task is something you can complete in one session. For example, I can't write a book in one session. However, I can perhaps write half of a chapter in one session, so I could regard each half chapter as one task.

Re-prioritise the list frequently, putting the most urgent tasks at the top and the least urgent tasks at the bottom. When you complete a task, delete it or move it to an archive of completed tasks. It's sometimes nice to look back over a long list of successfully completed tasks.

Weekly Plans

Have a way to plan your week. I have a document with days of the week across the top and 'Morning / Afternoon / Evening' down the side. I maintain two of these: one for the current week and one for next week. These are the only weeks I feel I need to plan in detail. My diary and 'To do' list suffice for everything else.

I regularly check my 'To do' list so I know which tasks I need to complete. I then allocate these tasks to my plan for this week or next. Of course, there are times when unexpected events disrupt fine plans and good intentions! Nonetheless, being as organised as you can be is better than not being organised at all.

A Filing Cabinet

Get a filing cabinet and some folders to go in it (these don't have to be expensive). Create one folder for everyone you do business with and arrange them alphabetically. If anyone ever pays you money, or you pay them, that person or organisation should be in a file in your filing cabinet.

Don't let a small mountain of unopened envelopes and correspondence build up waiting to be filed. Deal with correspondence when it comes in. If you need it, file it. If you don't, throw it away.

Business Planning

In business terms, a plan is a goal with a timescale. The goals you set for yourself should be (a) ambitious and (b) realistic. If a goal is not both ambitious and realistic, then it's not worth having.

Think about the tasks you need to complete in order to achieve each goal. Put each of these tasks on your 'To do' list. Not only is this a sensible way to approach any goal, but smaller tasks look more achievable than big ones so it helps to keep you motivated.

Think about the resources you need to complete each task. Resources can include time, money, people (plus their knowledge and expertise), materials, tools and processes. If you have the resources you need, or can get them, great. If there are things you don't have and can't get, then you need to modify your plan accordingly. This is just common sense.

Budget

Having a budget is a very important aspect of being organised. However, many self-employed people, especially younger ones, tend to neglect it.

You can find free advice all over the internet about how to budget effectively and organise your finances. If you do nothing else, take the time to list all your essential weekly or monthly outgoings. This gives you a clear idea of how much money you need to earn to keep yourself out of debt.

If you're not making enough money, you need to either reduce your expenditure or increase your disposable income. This is the plain truth of the matter. To think you have any other option is to bury your head in the sand and ignore reality. Unfortunately, even if you try to ignore reality, reality won't ignore you.

This is one of the most important points in this book, especially if you're relatively young. It's great to have talent and ambition, but getting into debt is neither smart nor fun. The word 'budget' is your friend. Know what you can afford and what you can't. It makes your life a lot happier.

Now that we've looked at a few basic ways to get organised, what else can you do to be more productive?

Turn Off TV

Do you want to be more productive? To achieve great things for yourself? Make money, fulfil your potential and have good times?

If so, turn off your TV. Better still, get rid of it altogether (as I did a number of years ago). This is the best way I know to dramatically boost your productivity.

There are some great TV shows. However, most TV exists to stuff adverts into your mind. I doubt that any part of fulfilling your potential involves sitting mute and passive in front of a screen, with your brain switched off, so that other people can fire advertising into your head to create wealth for themselves. How is this going to get you anywhere?

If you ignore TV for the next five years, you'll be better off and get far more done. You will also keep your brain switched on, instead of regularly parking it in 'passive / absorb' mode while you watch other people do interesting things. Nothing bad will happen and you won't miss out. After five years, anything good that was on will still be around in the form of box sets, downloads and whatever else they invent.

Some people get worried about living without TV for a few years. They say things like, "We all need a bit of mindless relaxation now and again." This is open to debate — I'm not sure relaxation needs to be either 'passive' or 'mindless' and I can think of many more satisfying ways to spend my leisure time than staring at a TV. However, that's a discussion for another time. This part of the book is about ways to increase your productivity and ditching your TV is one of the simplest, best and most effective ways to do this.

Switch off your TV. Switch it back on again when you have all the wealth and success you can handle or when you're so old that watching TV is more or less all you can do. The good TV will still be around for you to enjoy. It's not going to vanish.

The Non-Singer Story

Having suggested that you switch off your TV, here's a rather sad true story. I once knew someone who had an administrative role in an office. She wasn't very happy. She wanted to be a singer or at least to work in the field of musical theatre and spend all day with singers, musicians and musical directors.

She knew that she should, and *could*, make some progress towards her goal. Her main complaint was that she just didn't have enough time.

This woman followed *four* soap operas every week. Each of these soap operas had multiple episodes. At a conservative estimate, she spent ten hours a week just watching soap operas, or roughly forty hours a month. Yet she claimed she didn't have any time to work towards her goal of a career in musical theatre.

Does this sound crazy? Yes. Does it also sound familiar? Probably, because many people live in a similar way. They complain they don't have time to change direction and fulfil their potential, yet they burn the time they *do* have on things that confer no benefit whatsoever, like passively staring at TV. It's not as if they're ever going to *stop* making soap operas.

Avoid The Internot

When people use the internet in a time-wasting, unproductive way, I refer to it as the 'internot'. As in, "I'm into not getting anything done". Don't waste time on the internot.

The internet is, of course, a wonderful resource and you should make good use of it whenever it's practical and constructive to do so. I use it all the time for research, learning and keeping in touch with friends all over the world. However, you can waste a vast amount of time online if you're not careful.

Stay focused on fulfilling your potential. You're not going to do this by spending countless hours online looking at funny cat videos or arguing with people you've never met about something in the news (it's not as if you're going to change anyone's mind). Arguing online is a complete waste of time. You might as well invent a U-shaped telescope.

Get Out Of Bed

If you want to be more productive, spend less time in bed. This means either getting up earlier or going to bed later.

The earlier you get up, the more wonderful hours you can devote to completing various tasks. Yes, it's important to get enough sleep (as I say elsewhere in this book). But there's a difference between getting enough sleep and dozing away in bed when you could be making some progress with all your different projects. I've never met a successful person who said, "Well, the secret of my success is the truly vast amount of time I spent lazing in bed...".

Time-shift Your Attitude

Here's a little trick that may help you to become more productive. Realise that the way you feel about something *now* isn't necessarily how you'll feel about it later or under different circumstances.

It works like this. Let's say you're comfortable in bed one morning. You know you should get up but you feel rather content where you are and disinclined to move. You say to yourself, "Perhaps right *now* I don't feel like getting up. But that's not how I'll feel once I'm up, enjoying my morning shower, enjoying the splash of the water on my face and thinking about all the stuff I'm going to get on with today."

Here's another example. Suppose you've been putting off doing some important paperwork, such as your annual accounts. Say to yourself, "Right *now*, I don't feel like getting this done. But I'll feel different once I've actually started and I'm making some progress. I'll really enjoy getting it out of the way and knowing I can cross it off my 'To Do' list."

This is a simple way to manage your own feelings and overcome those occasional 'I just don't feel like it' moods.

Take Time Off

If you want to get a lot done, learn to take time off.

If you want to be highly productive, this doesn't mean working all hours of the day, burning yourself out so you feel weary and fatigued on a regular basis. This is a disastrous strategy and you will almost certainly make yourself ill. Nobody makes a lot of progress from sick bay. Learn to take regular breaks, have some 'rest and relax' time and do some stuff that's just for fun.

Whereas some people have to learn the discipline of working, self-employed people often have to learn the discipline of *not* working! When you work for yourself, there's always something to do, always another thought rolling around inside your head. It's easy to fall into the trap of working non-stop. Learn to have some leisure and pleasure time to avoid burning out.

Clearly, it's important to get the balance right. Too much time off is just as harmful to your progress as too little. It may take you a while to achieve the ideal balance.

Beyond The Basics

In this chapter, I've offered you some basic advice about productivity. Needless to say, I have only scratched the surface of what is actually a vast and fascinating subject. If you want to learn more about personal productivity, there are many books you can read and systems you can learn about. I'd like to mention a couple of options that come highly recommended by people I know.

Some of my friends recommend 'Getting Things Done', a 'total work-life management system' developed and pioneered by David Allen. It is commonly abbreviated to GTD. The success of Allen's original GTD book has spawned a range of corresponding software and apps, such as OmniFocus and Doit.im. You may like to check it out.

I also know people who like the ideas in 'The 4-Hour Workweek' by Tim Ferriss, a hugely successful book that has, inevitably, spawned a few sequels. Have a look if you think it sounds appealing.

All I ask is that you don't make the mistake of thinking that buying a book or a bit of software will, on its own, make any difference.

* * *

What's Next?

There are some common blocks that tend to get in the way of success and productivity. In the next section we'll look at how to overcome a few of them, including the perfect solution for procrastination!

8. Dealing With Common Blocks

"In order to live free and happily you must sacrifice boredom. It is not always an easy sacrifice."

— Richard Bach

8. Dealing With Common Blocks

In this chapter I want to discuss six common blocks to self-fulfilment and suggest some ways to deal with them.

Block #1: Fear

There are two types of fear: healthy fear and destructive fear. Healthy fear is part of your natural survival instincts. It's what stops you from walking too near the edge of cliffs. Destructive fear is neither good nor useful and is one of the commonest blocks to self-fulfilment. You can learn destructive fears from many sources such as bad experiences, bad examples set by other people, emotional scars and bruises and scare-mongering tales in the media.

I can't give you an easy fix for all destructive fears. What I can offer are four words that might help: nothing bad will happen.

Nothing Bad Will Happen

Whenever you feel fear, ask yourself which kind of fear it is: healthy or destructive? If it's destructive, you have learned it from a bad experience, from someone else or from a source that's trying to exploit and manipulate you. Ask yourself whether you'd prefer to keep hold of it, so it will continue to stifle your potential, or let it go? Maybe you'll decide to let it go, given that you never wanted it, you don't need it and it's not doing you any good.

When you fear something, you are choosing to imagine that a future situation will have a harmful outcome. For example, you are choosing to imagine that an important meeting will go badly. In effect, you are frightened of your own imagination. It's *your* imagination, so why not use it in a good way? Use it so that it *helps* you instead of holding you back. Imagine the situation going well and leading to a happy result or at least a perfectly safe one. Just take a moment to say to yourself, "Nothing bad will happen" and realise that you have no reason to think otherwise. Imagining a good outcome is just as valid as imagining a bad one so you may as well exercise that preference.

I am not advocating being *reckless*. Remember, I have made the distinction between healthy fear (which keeps you safe) and destructive fear (which holds you back). I'm a fan of healthy fear since I like surviving and being free from injury. But ditch the destructive fear. Remember: "Nothing bad will happen."

***

Dare To Fail, Dare To Be Bad

A very common fear is the fear of failure. More specifically, the fear of public failure. Nobody likes the notion of trying something in front of other people and getting it wrong. This affects everyone in the performing arts when they are just starting out and many other people as well. What if I try this business venture and I make lots of mistakes? What if I try selling my products but I find I'm not very good at selling?

The answer to this kind of fear is to make your peace with reality. You cannot start a journey at the end. You cannot be experienced without gaining experience. The only way to have done something a hundred times is to have done it the first time. So, just go through the learning curve, accept it as an unavoidable necessity and enjoy your journey of discovery and improvement. Dare to fail so you eventually succeed. All successful people have had to do this.

Even if you try and fail, you can give yourself more credit than those who don't even try. For more on this point, see 'The BITDIG Principle' later in this book. Also, read 'Black Box Thinking' by Matthew Syed. It will give you a completely new way to think about so-called 'failure'.

Find A Safe Place

One good way to deal with fear is to use safe places. When you're learning something new, find a safe arena in which you can practice without bad consequences. If you're learning about selling, for example, call a few prospects who are *not* very important to your success. This means you'll be better when you call the ones who *are* important.

If you want to be a performer, do some small, local 'try out' gigs, or free charity shows, where the audience is small and it won't matter if you don't give the greatest performance in the world. This helps you to be better when you're doing a gig you really want to go well. Practise when the outcome *doesn't* matter so you're great when it *does*.

If You Need Help

It's not always easy to get rid of destructive fears. They can be burned pretty deeply into your system. There are therapists and counsellors who might be able to help you with fears that seem to be holding you back.

You may also want to look at a famous book by Susan Jeffers, called 'Feel The Fear And Do It Anyway'. She offers a lot of good advice and suggestions.

Block #2: Self-Pity

You know what self-pity sounds like: "Why is the world so unfair?";
"Why was I treated so badly?"; "How come there's no justice?". As a
self-employed person, you will most certainly have the opportunity to
feel this way from time to time. Sometimes you do everything right and
get nowhere while someone else, less deserving than you, walks off with
all the success and rewards.

I don't know any successful self-employed people that have much time
for self-pity. It's seriously unhelpful stuff and you should have as little to
do with it as possible.

There are at least three good ways to deal with it.

1. Be Realistic

Understand that the universe is completely indifferent to you. It doesn't
owe you anything and nobody promised life would be fair. If you are
having the type of day where the world is ignoring whatever you would
regard as fair, you can say, "Good, the world is behaving normally
today. Everything is as it should be."

As Mark Twain said, "Don't go around saying the world owes you a
living. The world owes you nothing. It was here first."

2. Have Some Perspective

Think of all the times in life when life's unfairness works *in your favour*.
Did you have access to clean drinking water today? Millions of people
don't have this luxury. They don't think it's very fair. Even if you have
some money troubles, you're probably not experiencing serious poverty
and hardship. Millions of people in the world live in great poverty every
day. They don't see anything very fair about it.

You have to be careful with this mode of thinking. To say you can't feel
down because some people are worse off than you is like saying you
can't be happy because someone else, somewhere in the world, is even
happier.

Indulging in self-pity doesn't serve any practical purpose. However, if
you *must* spend a while dwelling on how unfair life is, you may as well
look at both sides of the page and maintain a healthier perspective.
When you look around, you'll realise there are lots of ways in which the
unfairness works in your favour.

3. Ticket For The Titanic

That result you wanted and didn't get? Maybe it will turn out to be a good thing. You never know. Think of all the people who desperately wanted to get on the Titanic but couldn't get a ticket. Back in April 1912, I'm sure some of them were cursing their luck and saying, "It's so unfair!"

It's easy to kid yourself that you know what would be a good result or a bad one, but it's awfully hard to be sure. Marilyn Monroe used to sing a song about it: 'After You Get What You Want You Don't Want It'.

Let's say you're a young actor in Hollywood auditioning for a part in a movie. You are perfect for the role and you desperately hope they'll choose you. The role is great and you expect it will lead to success, fame and fortune. You do a great audition but you don't get the part. They give it to someone who isn't as good as you and who hasn't worked as hard as you have. Time for a bit of self-pity, right? Well, maybe not. Maybe the actor who got the part will have a terrible time working on that movie. Maybe, despite all the hype and expectations, the movie will tank and effectively kill the career of everyone involved. It happens.

Indulge in self-pity if you want. I think you'll find it's a poor substitute for having a laugh, realising you don't know what would have happened, saying 'Ticket for The Titanic' under your breath and getting on with something else.

Block #3: Self-doubt

So far, we've looked at two great blocks to self-fulfilment and personal success: fear and self-pity.

The third one is self-doubt.

In a way, I've actually already dealt with this. It more or less works the same way as fear. I explained that there is healthy fear, which serves the rather useful purpose of keeping you alive, and destructive fear, which is useless junk you may as well get rid of. Similarly, there is healthy self-doubt and destructive self-doubt.

If you are given a particular task and you lack any relevant knowledge and experience, your sense of self-doubt is actually very useful. Never take part in a trapeze act unless you've done the training. Don't try to defuse a bomb unless you know what you're doing. However, there is also destructive self-doubt, which is a kind of emotional injury. The way to deal with it is very similar to how I suggested you deal with fear. Ask yourself *how* you gained the self-doubt or *why* you acquired it. Was it because people said horrible things to you when you were younger? Were you mocked, criticised, told that you're not good enough? Or did you just go through a few experiences of 'failure' and decide there was something inadequate about you?

Have a think about where the self-doubt comes from and then realise that you didn't ask for it, you don't want it and you don't have to carry it around with you anymore. You can leave it in the past, where it belongs, and live the rest of your life without it.

Lies And Impostors

Here's another way to look at it: your behaviour can either be life-affirming or lie-affirming. Imagine that someone calls you a loser. If you believe them, you'll start to behave as if you really are a loser. It's a lie (you're not a loser at all) but the way you behave starts to affirm the lie. Never let your behaviour become lie-affirming. Always behave in a way that is life-affirming.

A specific type of self-doubt is what's known as 'impostor syndrome'. Some people, when they begin to enjoy a bit of success, can't escape the nagging suspicion that they are a bit of a fraud. There's an internal voice that says: "This success is a fluke and all the praise is misplaced. I'm not as good as people think. I'm an impostor and I'll soon be found out. People will realise I'm no good and I'll never work again."

Impostor syndrome probably has a range of fascinating emotional and psychological causes, none of which I'm qualified to discuss. All I will point out is this: to be an impostor you have to *knowingly* and *intentionally* engage in deceit and misrepresentation. This is what the word means. By definition, you cannot *unintentionally* be an impostor. If you're not deliberately lying to anyone, and not trying to fake anything, then you're entitled to any work, money or praise that comes your way.

Self-doubt is nasty, toxic stuff, so let me tell you the truth. If you try to be good to yourself and to others, then you're fine. There's nothing wrong with you and no reason to doubt yourself at all. What's more, you're a wonderful, likeable person and terrific just as you are.

I believe in you. Millions of others would believe in you too, if you just gave them a chance to do so. You can't change the past, but no-one can stop you from changing the future. It's your future and you can put whatever you want in it. You can fill it with self-doubt if you want. I think you'd be better off fizzing with bright, warm love for yourself and your potential, love for others and love for life.

Choose The Voice You Use

In this section I've already mentioned issues such as self-doubt and self-pity. If you struggle with these and other aspects of self-confidence, you may like to know about a very helpful question you can ask yourself every now and again. Here's the question: "Which voice am I using right now?"

When you talk to yourself (either internally or out loud) you can use any one of several different voices.

You can use a Victim Voice. "Everyone and everything's against me. People don't treat me the way they should. I've been wronged so many times I can't count them all."

You can also use the closely related Self-pity Voice. "Life's so unfair to me. I try so hard but have so little to show for it. It's just not right. I deserve better than this."

You can also choose to use your Hopeless Voice. "There's just nothing I can do about this situation. I don't have any options or choices, and I can't make it any better. The outlook is bleak."

You can use all of these different voices from time to time, if that's what you want. Personally, I can't see how any of them will help you to be successful or to live a fulfilled life. Can you?

Every time you use one of these voices, you create a loop. You hear yourself say something negative and this goes into your mind as fresh input. This, in turn, affects and shapes your attitude, leading you to think negative thoughts. When you express these thoughts, whether to yourself or out loud, you complete the loop.

Whichever voice you choose, it has consequences. For example, consider the Self-pity Voice. As soon as you use this voice, you ignore the fact that you are the 'architect' of your life, so to speak, and you have at least some responsibility for where you've ended up. Self-pity says, "I'm the victim, not the agent".

This gets in the way of you doing something positive and productive about your situation. The Self-pity Voice doesn't just cloud how you feel about the past and how you came to be where you are. It also clouds the future, making you less inclined to plan your way forward. Once you've cast yourself in the role of helpless, passive victim, you're less likely to think, "Okay, so let me think about the steps I can take to get to a better place, to allow a better picture to emerge."

The fact is, you can choose which voice you use to express yourself. One good alternative is to use your Success Voice. "Right, let's figure out the steps I need to take to get from where I am to where I want to be, draw up a plan and take some positive action. If I can make a lot of progress, great. If I can only make a little bit of progress, that's better than none. If I can't make any progress at all right now, let's figure out how to get to a place where I can, and focus on that."

'Making progress' usually involves taking action, moving, getting out of your rut or your room and seeing other people. I've heard a lot of success stories. None of them sound like this: "I achieved all this by sitting in a chair at home, thinking about stuff and remaining rather inert."

When you use a different voice, you get different results.

Block #4: Procrastination

Many people who think they'd like to do their own thing tend to procrastinate and, as a result, never get anywhere. This is a shame, given that doing your own thing and making some money is fulfilling, hugely rewarding, lots of fun and gives you a real sense of achievement.

If you're prone to a lot of procrastination, let me offer some help.

The Perfect Solution

Here's the perfect solution to procrastination. Think about your main project, goal or ambition. This could be changing your career or main source of income, setting up a new business, making a significant change in your life or whatever else it happens to be.

Figure out whatever the date is two months from today. Make a note of it, put a red cross in your diary, draw a smiley face on your wall chart or whatever. At the end of those two months, if you have made some genuine, practical and significant progress towards your goal, and have some results to show, well done! You're well on your way.

If, at the end of those two months, you haven't taken *any* practical steps towards your goal, then forget it. Abandon the idea because it's never going to happen. You may be a wonderful human being in many ways but you probably aren't suited to self-employment and this book is not for you. The truth is, if self-employment is right for you, you will feel you *can't wait* to make some progress and turn your ideas into reality. The passion, the determination to make some progress will burn inside you so intensely that you feel you *must* take steps towards your goal.

If you haven't made any significant progress in two months, then two years or two decades wouldn't make any difference. It's not necessarily a bad thing to realise this. You may have saved yourself a lot of time.

That's my perfect solution to procrastination. You're welcome.

Let me add two notes of clarification. This 'two month deadline' idea applies to your *main* goal or project. I'm not referring to small, side projects that may not be all that important.

I'm also referring to procrastination, not pragmatism. Procrastination is the wasteful tendency to talk but never act. This is very different from setting a specific project aside for informed and pragmatic reasons. You may well have an idea you save in your 'For later' folder because you have other priorities. This isn't procrastination, just pragmatism.

More Thoughts On Beating Procrastination

Here are a few more thoughts on the subject.

Fear is a major source of procrastination — you don't take any practical steps forward because you're worried that things might not work out well. You need to get past this. First of all, stop worrying about making a mistake. Everyone makes mistakes and great people make great mistakes! As various wise people have pointed out over the years, "The person who never made a mistake never made anything."

Secondly, it's much better and more interesting to actually *do* something, and learn from the experience, than do nothing and have no experience to learn from. It's okay to fail now and again. So long as the sky doesn't fall in and nobody dies, it doesn't really matter. Whatever you try will lead either to success or learning. These are both good things.

Another aspect of procrastination is that you might sometimes find it hard to be decisive. Just remember this: the important decisions in your life *will* get made at some point. Your only choice is whether you make these decisions for yourself or you wait until they get made for you — by other people, by circumstances or simply by the passage of time.

I would respectfully suggest that you are the world's greatest living expert when it comes to making decisions about your life and how to live it. You are the number one, top-ranking expert in the entire world on this subject, almost as if you've been studying it your entire life. I therefore suggest you make you own decisions rather than wait for them to be made for you. Also, don't leave it too late to make decisions. You can't choose where to sit on a train that's left the station.

One final point about procrastination: remember that asking for advice is not the same as making some progress. Your mentor and other self-employed people are a valuable source of help and support but they don't like to waste their time. Self-employed people are keen to help *active* people with a genuine interest in achieving things and getting something done. However, they are very wary of people who just sit around speculating but never actually take any positive action or make any progress.

It only takes ten seconds to ask for advice. It takes ten minutes or ten hours to give it, according to the circumstances. Using up someone else's time isn't the same thing as getting something done. Get started, make something happen, have some work in progress to show. When you can demonstrate that you're actually making progress, and have taken some practical steps, you'll find other self-employed people more than willing to offer a bit of advice and guidance. They can see that you're actively doing something, and producing results, as opposed to just speculating and procrastinating.

Block #5: What Other People Might Say

Many people who are contemplating working for themselves worry about what other people might say. In particular, they worry about what their partner, family or friends will say if they suddenly announce their decision to set up their own business, become a professional juggler or start offering life coaching.

Let me share a few thoughts about this.

First of all, don't waste much time on what you *imagine* other people might think or say. Until someone *actually* says something negative, it hasn't happened so it's not an issue. For all you know, you might find other people very supportive.

What if someone does say something disparaging? Well, I think it's a good idea to love them and to make allowance for their doubts — after all, they might not see the same potential that you see. They're allowed to say whatever they want and to have a different point of view. Don't respond angrily or get drawn into an argument. It's perfectly okay to want to fulfil your potential and to see where your talents can take you. If other people want to say a few negative things, maybe that's the best contribution they can make at the time. Their limitations don't have to be *your* limitations.

The only way to never get negative comments is to never do anything. Of course, you'll never get any positive comments either!

Spouse Or Partner

Clearly, if you're going to make any major changes in your life, particularly one that might affect your income, then you'll need to discuss it with your spouse or partner, if you have one. It's not as easy as saying, "If your partner loves you, they will want to support you." There's a bit more to it than that.

First of all, as I mention several times in this book, there is no such thing as job security. It's a myth, like a golden unicorn. You can believe in it if you want but there's no evidence that any such thing exists. Quite the opposite. As I outlined earlier in this book, we live in the age of magic technology which, though it's wonderful in many ways, inevitably means there are fewer jobs to go round.

Secondly, you only get one life, so you either fulfil your potential or you don't. Money is important but it isn't all that matters. Suppose you have a job you dislike and most of the time you're tired, stressed and in a bad mood. Is this the person your partner wants to be with and to see every day? Maybe they'd prefer it if you were happy, less stressed and doing something you actually believe in — even if, at first, there's less money coming in. Maybe you'd have a better relationship as a result.

I know a lot of self-employed people who are in happy, committed, long-term relationships. Fulfilling your potential doesn't mean you can't build a great relationship with someone. You don't have to be consigned to a job you hate, forever, just because you're worried what the person you love might say.

Family And Friends

Apart from your spouse or partner, you may be worried about what your family and friends will say if you decide to pursue the path of self-employment.

Friends are important in life but here's the difference between a real friend and a fake one: real friends believe in you and want to support you. If someone doesn't believe in you, they may be many things but they don't know how to be a real friend. Maybe it would be okay for you to see a little less of them.

It's also worth bearing in mind that some people make negative comments because they feel stuck in a miserable life and don't want to think you're on your way to a better one. For the sake of politeness and diplomacy, it's probably not a good move to mention this out loud. Just be ready to make allowance for it.

A highly effective response to negative comments and disparaging remarks is to quietly go ahead and be successful. Everyone who has enjoyed any sort of success can tell you stories of people who said very negative or hurtful things during the early stages of their career. Of course, those negative voices are nowhere to be found later on. They vanish into the silence they would have been better to preserve in the first place.

I can assure you I have friends who think it's a bit strange that companies pay me a lot of money to give talks, or that I have private VIP clients all over the world who pay me to be their coach and mentor. Yes, my friends sometimes tease me about it. Only the other day, a friend of mine said he couldn't understand why anyone would pay me to talk to them, although he could understand if they paid me to shut up!

Well, a little good-natured teasing never hurt anyone. The fact is, most of my friends these days are also self-employed so they believe in me just as I believe in them. They delight in my success just as much as I delight in theirs.

Block #6: The Grass Is Always Greener

Let me introduce you to two people, Adam and Ben, both in their early thirties. Similar backgrounds and aptitudes, similar office jobs. They both harbour aspirations to quit their job and do their own thing.

Adam has a wife and two young children. Ben is single and is only responsible for himself.

Adam says, "It's all right for *you*, Ben. You only have yourself to worry about. If you want to quit your job, you're a free agent and can do what you want. It's not quite so easy for me. I have a wife and two kids to worry about. I need the job security, I need to keep the money coming in. You can economise for a while but I've got mouths to feed. You can struggle for a bit if you have to while you build up a new business. I doubt my family would be happy if we suddenly had next to nothing. I wish I had it easy, like you."

Ben says, "It's all right for *you*, Adam. You've got your wife to support you. If you quit your job, maybe her salary will tide you over. Plus she can act as your manager, agent, assistant or anything else — whereas I have to do it all myself. Also, you have a ready-made workforce. If you need to stuff mailers into 200 envelopes, you can get the kids to help. I have to do it all myself or pay someone. What's more, emotional support counts for a lot. You've got your wife's support whereas I'm on my own. I wish I had it easy, like you."

It's perfectly possible for two sincere, thoughtful people to both believe the *other* one has the easy life. Hence the saying, "The grass is always greener on the other side". This kind of thinking can be a very effective block to positive action, often preventing people from living the life they want to lead.

Here's the truth. Whatever circumstances you imagine are holding you back, I can find someone who has all the same problems and constraints, and a few more besides, who has nonetheless taken the action that you're avoiding. It comes down to a simple choice: you can either blame your circumstances or shape them.

Every life is rich in details. Whatever choice you're considering, you can always find some aspects of your life that work in your favour and others that seem to work against you. Pros and cons, pluses and minuses. If you choose to only see advantages, that's all you'll see. If you choose to only see disadvantages, likewise.

It's the same for everyone. Don't go around thinking it's easier for everyone else and *you* are the one with all the problems and obstacles. The grass is equally green on both sides of the fence.

No-One Famous Ever Came From Here

In 1990, Lou Reed and John Cale released an excellent album called 'Songs For Drella'. It's one of the finest albums I've ever heard and you may want to give it a listen. The first track on the album, called 'Small Town', contains these lines:

"When you're growing up in a small town
You say no one famous ever came from here"

I think this conveys a particular type of 'greener grass' thinking that affects many people: they look around their small, humble home town and feel it's unlikely they'll ever lead much of a fulfilled life.

I can relate to this because it's precisely how I used to think throughout my childhood years. Though I currently live near London, I grew up in a small town in the north-west of England called Bolton. It was a pleasant enough place but to me it always felt like a small, insignificant part of the world where nothing very notable ever happened. Though I was interested in show business in my teens, I was convinced that nobody famous or successful could ever come from a small town like mine. I used to think that if only I lived somewhere more exciting, with more opportunities, I'd stand a much better chance of doing something interesting with my life.

Of course, I was completely wrong about this. At the time of writing this book, I can think of at least three very successful people in this country who come from Bolton. Peter Kay is the most commercially successful comedian in the country, able to sell out giant stadium venues. Vernon Kay is a very successful TV presenter while Amir Khan is a world champion boxer. (Evidently, the key to success is to come from Bolton and have a surname beginning with 'K'.)

It's not where you come from that matters, but where you're going. You don't choose the start of your journey, but you do get to choose the direction and the destination.

* * *

What's Next?

The next section consists of a few good ideas that will help your new venture to thrive, including a few interesting things to do with your mind!

9. Good Things To Do

"You can fix anything but a blank page."

— Nora Roberts

9. Good Things To Do

In one sense, every self-employed person's life is the same: you always have lots of things to do and never enough time to do them. Whether you're trying to run a new semiconductor factory or develop your career as a stage hypnotist, you'll find that the bucket of things to do is always bigger than the time bucket.

I think this indicates a serious flaw in the way the universe has been constructed. We should campaign for bigger time buckets so we can all get everything done properly, in a relaxed way and without rushing. I'd start the campaign myself but, well... I just don't have the time.

Until this regrettable error is fixed, you can be certain that not having a big enough time bucket will be part of your self-employed experience. This being the case, I've no wish to burden you with long lists of things you should do. However, permit me to suggest a small number of things that I believe will make your working life significantly easier.

Note that I am not suggesting these things will make your working life *easy*. Self-employment is never easy. Talk to self-employed people about having an easy life and they'll just laugh in your face. I don't know any self-employed people who have an easy life or would particularly want one. What they want is a *fulfilled* life, which is a very different creature. Nonetheless, you can make your life a little *easier*.

Make Connections

In the section on setting up your business, I mentioned the importance of finding a mentor. In this context, a mentor is someone who is already doing what you want to do, seems pretty good at it, has a positive outlook and is willing and able to offer the benefit of their experience. I am intentionally repeating the point because it's so important.

If you want to work for yourself, find a mentor either in real life or online. Say you'd to keep in touch, have a chat from time to time, ask a few questions and get the benefit of their advice. Talking to someone who already has years of relevant experience will save you a lot of time, money and wasted effort. They are a long way ahead of you on the learning curve so it makes sense to take their advice where possible.

Even if you can't find a mentor, make an effort to connect with as many self-employed people as you can. As well as being able to offer you help and support, they are the only people who can appreciate the various challenges involved in being self-employed.

A Bad Mistake

Here's one of the worst decisions I've ever heard of.

John was a successful comedian with ten years' professional experience and a full diary. He worked the comedy circuit but also got a lot of private bookings. This was exactly the sort of career that Ken, a beginner, wanted to have. (These are not their real names.)

They became friends and John offered to help Ken. He invited Ken to come along to a few gigs and helped him with his material. John even said, "I'll refer some clients to you so you get some work and a chance to build up your name, in return for 20% commission." Ken rejected this offer, saying he didn't want to pay any commission and would rather get his own work.

This was a bad mistake. If someone with ten years of relevant experience is offering to help you and give you work, the right response is to say yes, grab the opportunity with both hands, keep on very good terms with that person and thank your lucky stars.

Use The Internet

Earlier in this book, I warned you against the perils of the 'internot', or wasting so much time online that your productivity suffers. That said, when you start working for yourself it *is* a good idea to use the internet and social media to your advantage. Just don't let it soak up too much of your time. How much is too much? Well, if you're unsure what month it is, your dog has given up on you and you're developing rickets… you might want to spend a little less time online.

The internet is the stuff of magic and miracles, and it's great to be alive in this amazing age of digital sorcery. Nonetheless, try to use the internet productively rather than let it soak up all your time. Educate yourself about using social media to successfully promote your business. There are plenty of free online guides if you look for them. There are also some excellent consultants who will handle your online marketing for you if you wish.

Creating a simple website that tells people about your business is, by itself, unlikely to bring in much work. However, it's worth having so you can refer people to it. Having an *e-commerce* website, designed to sell products and make money, is a different matter. Learning how to create e-commerce sites, and build a passive income, is one of the best favours I ever did for myself. Setting up an e-commerce site is beyond the scope of this book but is definitely a great option to explore. Just be warned: it's not easy, it takes time and it involves a *lot* of work!

Look After Your Body

I mentioned health and fitness in the section about getting yourself ready for self-employment. I'm returning to the subject because taking care of your health, both physically and mentally, is definitely a good thing to do if you want to be successful.

Take the best care you can of your body, which means taking regular exercise and being careful and thoughtful about what you eat. Don't ignore the benefits of simple things like learning to breathe properly and keeping yourself adequately hydrated. If you have any problems with this aspect of life, you may want to check out one of my websites: www.theaddictionfixer.com . You'll find plenty of help and information there.

When you keep yourself fit, you don't just increase your chances of staying healthy. You also tend to have a more dynamic approach to life and get more done. There's a strong correlation between being fit and being productive.

Being fit also means you can relax properly and you get far more benefit from your rest and your sleep. The resting heart rate of a fit person is significantly lower than that of someone who isn't fit.

Fitness also helps you to look your best and for many self-employed people looks can be important. If you're going to work for yourself, the way you look will affect how people respond to you, which in turn affects your ability to build rapport, sell and negotiate. If you're a performer or an entertainer, it clearly helps to look as good as you can. You don't get to choose whether you're blessed with good looks. You *do* get to choose whether you make the best of what you've got. Everyone looks better if they're fit and healthy, enjoy regular exercise, eat good food and get plenty of sleep.

Prevention Is Better Than Cure

For the benefit of younger people reading this book, let me be emphatic about one point: when it comes to health and fitness, prevention is *much* better than cure.

If you let yourself get fat and unfit, it will take some time and a bit of effort to undo the damage, lose the weight and get fit again. It's much better to just not let the problem develop in the first place. If you start smoking, you'll find it a bit challenging to quit later on. It's far easier and more intelligent to just not start in the first place. It's just money up in smoke and you're missing out on nothing.

The Biggest Killer: Stress

Another reason to either get or stay fit is that fitness is the antidote to stress, which is the biggest killer of all.

This section is about good things to do and it's a *really* good idea to protect yourself from stress. Learn how to deflect and defuse it. There are many ways to do this in addition to maintaining your physical fitness. For example, meditation and learning how to breathe correctly can both be very helpful.

There are also many activities that can reduce stress and anxiety. I find that playing my guitar, even for just a few minutes, is a great stress reliever. I discovered I can *either* feel stressed *or* play my guitar, but not both. Maybe you could find a similar activity that turns off the 'stress' circuits and helps to calm your mind and your spirit.

Laughter also helps. Read some funny stuff. Watch a few funny videos online. Meet up with a friend and have a good laugh at the ridiculous state the world is in (it's not as if you'll ever be short of material). It's a great way to relieve feelings of stress and worry.

If you have a serious problem with stress, find a therapist or counsellor who can help you. Hint: the idea is to do this *before* stress kills you.

Ignore 'Hedonistic' Celebs

A few celebrities project a rather effortless, carefree image, as if they're always partying, drinking and indulging in everything it's possible to indulge in. Impressionable people sometimes look at these celebrities and think, "They're living a wild, indulgent sort of life, but they look pretty good and seem to be having a great time! I'm going to follow their example!"

Here's the truth. The 'wild party animal' routine is more often than not just part of that particular celebrity's public persona. In reality, when nobody's looking, most of these people get up early, work out, watch what they eat and make sure they get enough sleep. Away from the cameras and media attention, most of them tend to be fairly health conscious. They know this is an important part of enjoying success and longevity, not to mention looking as good as they can.

Don't confuse their public persona for reality. A carefully crafted story fed to the media is not real life. That 'crazy party animal' is probably very different when there are no reporters, cameras or microphones around.

Look After Your Mind

As well as looking after your body and your physical health, take good care of your mind.

Your mind can do wonderful and impressive things. It can come up with great ideas, absorb knowledge, solve problems and distil wisdom from experience. Use your mind well and self-employment becomes a lot easier. I'm going to break this section down into four areas: Feed, Stimulate, Clear and Rest.

Feed Your Mind

You wouldn't want to have stopped learning at the age of ten — there was still a lot of good stuff for you to discover. The same is true if you're twenty years old, or forty, or eighty-three. If you don't feed your mind, it doesn't grow so you remain stuck, glued to one spot and one outlook. This is why I think it's a smart move to sample many different ideas, views and opinions.

If you like reading, read fiction and non-fiction, both old and new. Enjoy the writers you like and try a few you think you *won't* like — once in a while you'll be pleasantly surprised. If a friend mentions a book they're enjoying, give it a try and see what you make of it. If you dislike reading, you can still sample a wide range of ideas and views: listen to audio books and podcasts, watch YouTube videos and TED talks, chat with people who've read a bit more than you and enjoy discussing different points of view.

Keep up with news and current affairs, even if this isn't one of your main interests. It pays to at least follow the main news stories of the day and stay informed about what's going on in the world. Being unaware of the major news stories of the day never impresses anyone.

Feeding your mind in this way confers many benefits. For one thing, you'll pick up good ideas. Not all books are great but if you get even one good idea from a book, that's one good idea you didn't have before so you're better off.

If you're going to work for yourself, being aware of many different ideas and points of view is a real advantage. If there's nothing in your mind except last night's movie and the same ideas you had ten years ago, I think you'll struggle. I don't know many self-employed people who are 'intellectuals', as such. However, the vast majority enjoy the interplay of ideas, views and perspectives. Put simply, I don't know many people who think it's great to be empty-headed and devoid of ideas.

Stimulate Your Mind

As well as feeding your mind, keep it stimulated so it doesn't stagnate and decay.

Read about ideas that challenge your current outlook. If you only read what you already know and agree with, you can't learn anything. Learn about 'critical thinking' and how to avoid thinking errors and fallacies. You're going to be making lots of decisions as you build your business. It helps if you can tell good reasoning from bad.

Take in many different points of view and perspectives. Now and again, take an interest in subjects or areas you've never given much time to before. Try to see what other people find so interesting or fascinating about this or that subject. Search out good sources of wit and clever humour. Some comedians are very good at helping you to see things in different ways or from an unusual point of view.

Another good way to stimulate your mind is to tackle puzzles, crosswords and quizzes or to play games that give your mental muscles a good workout, such as chess (although I much prefer the ancient Japanese game of Go).

Clear Your Mind

It's a good idea to de-clutter your mind on a regular basis.

If there are things you need to remember, write them down so you don't have to carry them around in your head. Give your memory as little work to do as possible.

When ideas come to you, or you remember things you meant to see to, write them down or dictate them into a voice recorder so you don't clog up your mind.

If there are things you're worried or anxious about, talk them over with a friend or think about the best and worst case scenarios and write them out so you can release them from your mind. Don't let negative thoughts fester in your head for days on end.

In general terms, don't treat your mind like an infinitely elastic storage cupboard into which you constantly dump more and more clumps of information. This doesn't work and leads to problems. You'll forget some things and lose sleep over others. Clearing your mind helps you to focus on whatever tasks or projects you're working on. It also helps you to relax, rest and sleep well.

Rest Your Mind

You know that rest is important for your body. Even if you really like exercising, you wouldn't want to exercise all the time because you'd soon get exhausted. It's always better to balance exercise with rest.

It's the same with your mind. It needs proper rest or you'll soon reach the point of mental and emotional exhaustion. Regular meditation is really helpful. It helps you to stay calm and is a great way to stay focused on your values, goals and priorities.

In addition, always make sure you get enough sleep. Sleep is wonderful stuff: it's when your mind clears out junk and resets itself (a process we experience as dreaming) and your body heals, repairs and restores itself. I've already mentioned the notion of clearing your mind. Doing this before you go to bed can really help you to get a good night's sleep.

If you need help with aspects of your physical, mental and emotional health, get it from counsellors, therapists and other self-employed people who specialise in these areas.

Use ABC

Since this chapter is all about good things to do, I must mention the notion of ABC: Attitude, Behaviour, Consequences.

Your *attitude* towards any future event or challenge affects your *behaviour* which in turn affects the likely outcome or *consequences*.

Let's say Jill has an exam coming up and her attitude is, "This is an extremely tough exam and I probably won't pass." Given this attitude, she probably won't prepare very well for the exam or devote much time to it as she has largely convinced herself it's a waste of time. This attitude has predictable consequences and becomes a self-fulfilling prophecy.

Suppose Jill's attitude is like this: "Maybe it's a tough exam but this just means I'll get a great sense of achievement when I pass it! My chances are just as good as anyone else's and I may as well give myself the best chance I can of doing well. I'm going to study the syllabus, plan my study schedule and give it my best shot!" She is now far more likely to do well.

The same applies to anything else in life: going for a job interview, asking someone out, managing a large project, learning a new skill or making any significant change. Attitude affects Behaviour affects Consequences. It's as simple as ABC.

Dress To Impress

Another good thing to do, especially if you want to be a performer or entertainer, is to dress well and develop a bit of fashion sense.

I won't say a lot about this because, as anyone who knows me will readily testify, it's not exactly my strong point. I've never really cared much about self-presentation and what I know about style and fashion would fit on a sequin with room to spare.

Nonetheless, I will just pass on one excellent piece of advice to men reading this book. If you want to know what looks good on you, and how to look your best, ask a female friend for a little bit of advice and guidance. Broadly speaking, every woman in the world has already forgotten more than you'll ever know about style, fashion, colour, texture, what works and what doesn't.

Moreover, women are usually more than happy to help. Ask a female friend to go with you on a couple of shopping trips and give you a bit of advice about looking your best. It can be good fun and you'll be delighted by the results.

Do Some Charity Work

It's a good idea to do some charity work. I don't mean just give some money to a charity or worthy cause, although that's a good idea too. I mean actually give up some of your time to help out with whatever work they need people to do. You can easily search online for any charities or projects in your area that are looking for volunteers. I can promise that, whatever type of voluntary work you choose to do, you will be given a very warm welcome.

There are several reasons to do this. First of all, you'll feel great. You won't know what 'feel-good factor' really means until you've given up some of your own time and labour to help people less fortunate than yourself. Secondly, it's always a very educational experience. It will give you insights you wouldn't otherwise have and a broader perspective on life and society. It also means you get to meet people that you probably wouldn't meet otherwise.

Let me add one point of clarification. 'Doing some charity work' does not mean supplying your goods or services free of charge, especially if you're an entertainer. With rare exceptions, this is not a good idea. As a general rule, maintain a clear distinction between (a) the sort of work you normally expect to get paid for, and (b) the sort of work you're willing to do for a charity or good cause. Keep them separate.

Travel As Much As You Can

Here's another good idea: travel as much as you can. It gives you a better perspective on life, educates you, leads to interesting experiences and is (almost always) a lot of fun. As a wise friend once said, "Travel is the only thing where you spend money and come back richer."

'Travel' is a broad term that you can interpret as you wish. Some people prefer to travel alone while others like to travel in a group or with friends. Some want to explore their own region or country while others (like me) want to roam the entire world. I strongly recommend that you discover whatever kind of travelling suits you and pursue it as much as you can. Yes, there are some practical and financial limitations. Nonetheless, pursue every travel opportunity that comes your way. It confers many benefits and leads to wonderful experiences and memories.

Some Favourite Places

Travelling is not only one of my great passions but also one of my weaknesses. My friends and clients know that a really good way to get me to agree to anything (well, almost anything) is to lure me with a tasty travel opportunity! I've been fortunate enough to visit many wonderful places around the world that I'll remember forever. Just for fun, here are some of my favourites in no particular order.

The Hagia Sophia, Istanbul. The most incredible and mesmerising structure I have ever been inside. Quite breathtaking in terms of its size, scale, history and architecture.

Milford Sound, New Zealand South Island. The most spectacular scenery I have ever seen and a photographer's paradise.

The Kiluea Caldera, Volcano National Park, Hawaii. Stunning and emotionally overwhelming. Watch the planet smoulder with anger!

Easter Island. Home of the famous 'moai' or unique giant stone statues. A wonderful, magical place to visit (and I chose to go there at Christmas just because I thought this was funnier.)

Komodo Island. Home of the incredible Komodo Dragons, the largest lizards in the world. Seeing these incredible creatures 'up close and personal' is a remarkable experience by any standards.

Hiroshima Peace Memorial Park. No words can adequately describe the experience of visiting this part of the world, with its unique emotional sense of both tragedy and peace.

The Grand Canyon, Colorado, US. An obvious choice. Majestic, incredible, overwhelming, beautiful and easy to enjoy.

Cappadocia, Turkey. One of the strangest and most surreal landscapes in the world and completely captivating.

The Batu Caves, Gombak, Selangor, Malaysia. Malaysia is one of my favourite countries and the Batu Caves are simply extraordinary, especially if you visit during the feast of Thaipusam.

Torino, Italy. Tourists understandably flock to Rome, Florence and Pisa, all of which are wonderful. But I love Torino too, especially the view from the Piazza Vittorio Veneto looking across the river towards the Chiesa della Gran Madre di Dio.

Atomium, Belgium. A unique structure, in terms of imagination, design and engineering. I'm delighted to have presented one of my corporate lectures inside this amazing venue.

Iguazu Falls. Visually stunning, endlessly beautiful and magnificent in every way. The tours are well organised and highly enjoyable.

Petra, Jordan. The ancient stone city, carved from the rock of the desert. One of the most amazing and enchanting places I've ever seen.

Las Vegas. Despite the fact that I have no interest in gambling, I love Vegas and have thoroughly enjoyed every single one of my dozen or so visits.

* * *

What's Next?

If you want your new business to survive, there's one thing that can make a huge, positive difference. It's not something you can buy so you're going to have to build it yourself — but it's not something you can see or touch. What is it? I'll reveal all in the next chapter!

10. Build Your Network

"I'm a success today because I had a friend who believed in me and I didn't have the heart to let him down."

— Abraham Lincoln

10. Build Your Network

There's a hard way to go on your self-employed journey and a much easier way.

The hard way is to proceed alone. I literally don't know a single person who has managed to do this successfully (nor would I particularly want to). The easier way is to enjoy the support and help of other self-employed people. This is the option that I highly recommend.

Here are some good ideas about building your network of like-minded people.

Reach Out To People

It's a very good idea to connect with other self-employed people so you gradually build up your network. There are lots of ways to do this via social media groups, local clubs and societies, word-of-mouth and friend-of-a-friend connections.

You'll get good energy from other self-employed people (especially ones who have managed to achieve a little success) and they're also usually good fun to know.

My personal belief, based on past experience, is that you'll find other people who work for themselves far more helpful and fun to know than people who don't, for three reasons:

1. They're more effective. They tend to be efficient and get things right.

2. They understand your situation a lot better. They can relate to the various challenges you face in a way that other people cannot and they tend to be good at solving problems.

3. They tend to be more resourceful and have a broader range of contacts. In my experience, people in regular jobs may have a large *number* of contacts but self-employed people have a greater *variety* of contacts.

One of the very best aspects of my life is the number of wonderful, impressive self-employed people I know, all around the world. They are all very talented and good at what they do but they are also kind, helpful and fun to hang out with. I'm glad that the internet and miracles like Skype and Zoom make it so easy to keep in touch.

Build Credibility And Respect

Whatever your particular field happens to be, always be ready to share your work with your peers and to show people what you can do. It's the only way to establish credibility and build peer group respect. This is particularly important if you want to be an entertainer or build your business around your creative talent. Always be willing to show people what you can do. If you don't share, they won't care.

Never be reluctant to share your work just because you're a beginner. We all have to start somewhere! It's okay to say, "Well, I'm only a beginner so this may not be very good, but here's something I've been working on…". Those with more experience than you will give you plenty of help and encouragement for the simple reason that they were once beginners themselves.

Share your work and build your credibility. Peer group respect is a wonderful thing that opens doors and leads to enduring friendships.

Don't Judge On Looks

When building your network, don't judge people on their looks. It's nice that some people are charmingly handsome or outstandingly beautiful. Nonetheless, looks don't tell you much. They certainly don't indicate anything about character, capability or effectiveness.

Some people in my network are blessed with good looks. Some are not. However, they're all terrific people who are excellent at what they do, dependable, kind and helpful. You can't judge results by a face.

Collaboration Is Good

Earlier on in this book, I advised you not to set up your business in partnership with someone else. In my view, backed up by a couple of decades of experience, it's far better to be the sole owner of your business or company. However, *collaborating* with other self-employed people on specific projects is a great idea. Always look for opportunities to work with other people to your mutual advantage. It can lead to some fascinating work and is usually great fun as well.

Just be careful about the money! Always deal with other people on what's called a 'sunshine' basis: there's plenty of light and everyone can see clearly. Everyone has all the details about the revenue, the costs, how much money comes in, how much goes out and who gets what. Sunshine deals are good deals.

Youth And Experience

Having mentioned working together, there's one particular type of collaboration that I'd like to mention.

Two of the greatest things in life are youth and experience. Sadly, the more you have of one, the less you have of the other. This is just one of life's little twists. In your dealings with other people, especially other self-employed people, it's often worth exploring the possibility of a useful collaboration. What follows does involve some broad generalisations but I think they are sufficiently accurate for the point I'm trying to make.

If you have youth, you have health, vitality, energy and stamina, and you probably still look pretty good (or at least better than you will twenty years from now). You can lift heavy boxes, work long hours and absorb new ideas easily. You also understand modern technology. The only problem is that you lack life experience so you might seem a bit naive to older people.

If you have plenty of life and work experience, you have good judgment and perspective, a balanced outlook and the insight that comes from having made lots of mistakes. On the other hand, you don't have the energy you once had and you can't take your health for granted. In the eyes of younger people, you'll often seem laughably out of touch, especially with regards to technology, social trends and popular culture.

In the self-employed world, there's often an opportunity for Youth to help Experience and vice-versa. Rather than despising one another, Youth and Experience can work together in a very productive way. Spot these opportunities and be ready to capitalise on them.

Be Good PR For One Another

Be a good Public Relations officer and Cheerleader for other self-employed people and they'll (usually) return the favour. It costs nothing yet everyone benefits. I polish your halo for you, you polish mine and in everyone's eyes we get to shine.

When you work with other people, say good things about them. Post nice 'thank you' messages on social media saying how brilliant they are at what they do and what a great time you had working with them. You never know who might see your message and decide to hire your friend. Similarly, in social situations, say complimentary things about the other self-employed people present whenever a suitable opportunity arises. Make it your business to spread positive messages and boost their reputation a little. They'll do the same for you.

Offer Commission

A friend does you a favour and passes on a tip that means you get some work. They don't ask for money and none is discussed. They are happy to help.

When you've been paid, offer them some sort of payment or commission. They will probably just politely decline, saying something like, "Forget it, I was happy to help. Let's just say you can buy me a coffee next time we're in town." Nonetheless, make the offer.

If you make the offer, even if it's politely declined, you're showing your gratitude and a bit of business sense. After all, it's normal to pay commission to an agent or anyone who gets you some work. If you don't make the offer, you could get a reputation as someone who just takes other people's help and kindness for granted. This isn't good. In fact, it's a very good way to *discourage* people from doing you favours or offering assistance.

Learn About Other Self-employed Journeys

Learn what you can about other people who are doing their own thing (or trying to) and their stories. This is an important aspect of building up your network and it yields many benefits.

For one thing, you'll learn that even people you regard as highly successful made countless mistakes while they were building up their business or starting their career. Every success story is littered with bad choices, wrong turns and dead ends.

You will also discover that everyone, at some point or other, has had to contend with a storm of problems, struggles and setbacks. If you talk to even a handful of successful people, you'll soon understand that apathy, disdain and failure are the stuff success is made of. They all have stories to share of stony silence, blank indifference, awful gigs or clients and times when it seemed their entire business was about to collapse. Sharing these stories can be great fun and highly cathartic.

If nothing else, listing to other people's stories will help you to see that everyone goes through the same basic problems and difficulties. No-one gets a completely easy ride. However, great trials and tribulations can also be a valuable source of inspiration. Listening to other self-employed people will remind you that if you have the right outlook, get the product right and shout about it with admirable persistence, you'll generally emerge triumphant in the end. It might be a rocky road, but you'll get where you want to be.

Three Network Stories

I have mentioned elsewhere that self-employed people tend to be very good at getting things done and making things happen. To illustrate this point, here are three stories. The first two stories share some similarities. The third story puts the first two in perspective. All three stories are true.

Story #1: The Magic Show

My friend Lee Hathaway is one of the most talented and successful magicians in the country. There was another magician, called Paul, who did a great stage magic act that Lee wanted to see. Many of Lee's friends, myself included, also wanted to see Paul perform this particular act.

Lee found out that Paul was going to be passing through London and seized the opportunity. He contacted Paul and asked if he'd be willing to perform his act for a small, private audience if he (Lee) provided a suitable venue. Paul said yes.

Lee swung into action. He called a friend who runs a comedy club and got permission to use it for one Sunday afternoon. So, Lee had a venue.

Paul was going to need live musical accompaniment for his act. Lee gave his mate Shaun some money and said, "Go and buy an electronic keyboard." Then he phoned his friend Neil and said, "You can sight-read music, can't you? Good. Can you come along on Sunday afternoon and accompany Paul's act?" Neil readily agreed.

Next, Lee would need an audience. He called a friend who is a designer. Gave her the brief, got her to knock up a flyer he could hand out and put on Facebook. She did this in an hour.

To promote the event, Lee asked his friends who work as street entertainers to spread the word. He also made announcements on social media websites and got lots of his friends to do the same. It wasn't long before there was quite a 'buzz' about this one-off, special event!

Lee realised that Paul's act just on its own, great though it was, wouldn't be a full show. He therefore called a couple of other people, myself included, and said, "Hey, can you come along and do ten or fifteen minutes, just to pad the show out a bit?"

Lee made all this happen *in a few hours*. He could do this because he has a great network of self-employed people. The show went ahead and everything worked perfectly as planned. We all had a thoroughly enjoyable Sunday afternoon.

This is just one, small example of what self-employed people tend to be like. We have lots of skilled, talented and helpful friends so it's easy to get things done.

One more point about this story. In order to make all this happen, Lee had to be the sort of likeable person whose friends are willing to do him a favour. He had to have built up his network over many years and to have been a good friend to others when *they* asked for help.

Be a good friend. Build up your network. Earn people's respect and goodwill over time. It makes life easier and means you can make small miracles happen, like Lee creating this show out of nothing.

Story #2: The Haiti Benefit Night

In January 2010, a terrible earthquake struck Haiti. It caused a humanitarian disaster and an international relief effort began. I decided to organise a benefit event. My friend Jon immediately offered to be my co-organiser. We phoned a couple of possible venues, went to see one the next day and agreed a deal.

The venue we chose, while excellent in many ways, needed temporary staging plus sound and lighting equipment. Jon hit the phones and asked around. Within a week, he had secured everything we needed, arranged for delivery to the venue and found technicians to operate it.

We were going to need some acts. I contacted various friends and within a few days had a full line-up of top-class talent: singers, comedians, magicians, a juggler, a mind reader and a hypnotist. None of these people are famous but they are all superbly talented entertainers who excel in their respective fields.

There would be little point in organising this event if we didn't have an audience. Not a problem. I got two friends to set up a website where people could buy tickets for the show and also make donations to the cause. With other friends, we started to get the word out.

Jon and I decided to also have a charity auction on the night. We persuaded many people to donate gifts and prizes that we could auction off on the night. A couple of millionaires I know donated very valuable prizes indeed!

We wanted some souvenirs so Jon got a professional photographer to cover the event. I even got a professional cake-maker I know to donate a cake, decorated to fit the theme of the evening ('Magic Is Real'). People could buy slices of the cake, thereby raising more money.

On the night, the venue was full to capacity. My friend Neil and I hosted the show while Jon ran the technical side of things. The charity auction went well and everyone had a thoroughly good time. In one evening, we raised just under £5000 for the Red Cross.

Making all this happen took just *eighteen days*. Less than three weeks. This is what happens when self-employed people, especially performers and entertainers, work together.

Story #3: The Recruitment Ad

I was once doing some freelance work for a software company. They needed to place a recruitment advert in a magazine. I happened to see every step of this process because someone at a nearby desk was in charge of it.

First, a few people in the company had a series of meetings about this ad. These meetings led to further meetings in which the recruitment agency liaised with a design company and the marketing department to agree the content of the ad. The ad then had to be approved by about seven different people from various departments. Then someone had to prepare a contract and arrange payment before the ad could actually be submitted to the magazine. Just getting one ad placed in a magazine took about *five weeks* and involved several dozen people — a perfect example of slow, bloated bureaucracy.

Stories #1 and #2 show how things are done in the self-employed world.

Story #3 shows how things are done in the corporate world.

I know which I prefer.

* * *

What's Next?

The next section, which is all about good principles to follow, starts with a story about two musicians and ends with a James Bond villain!

11. Good Principles To Follow

"Failure is the condiment that gives success its flavour."

— Truman Capote

11. Good Principles To Follow

You may be wondering how to obtain a guarantee that working for yourself will end in success, wealth and widespread adulation.

Well, it's very simple. Just fill in the form on page 283 of this book, send it off and within days I'll send you a guarantee of resounding success for the rest of your life. There's no catch. It's a clear, simple guarantee of success that you can keep forever. It comes in a neat plastic frame in one of two colours: Spring Meadow Green or Clumsy Chef Red.

Of course, this isn't true. I can't provide you with this kind of guarantee and neither can anyone else. However, I can give you the next best thing: eight good principles to follow if you want to work for yourself. These may not guarantee success, but they do stack the odds dramatically in your favour.

Small, Simple, Humble

When you start working for yourself, I suggest you start small, start simple and start humble. Spend as little as you can and focus on whatever will bring in some money.

Don't worry about what you haven't got. Just do the best with what you *have* got (or can get).

Don't focus on things you can't do. There's always an infinite number of them and dwelling on them achieves nothing. Always focus on the things you *can* do, which is far more productive (so long as you transform thinking into doing.)

A few years ago, a friend of mine wanted to write and publish his own magazine. Unfortunately, he didn't have any of the usual tools for the job. He didn't have a computer, had never used a word processor and knew nothing about desktop publishing. What did he do? He got some paper, wrote and drew the entire magazine *by hand*, photocopied it and sold it! He successfully ran this magazine for several years.

Start small, simple and humble. Focus on what you have got, what you can do and what will bring in some money.

Prefer positive doing to positive thinking.

This is the very best advice I can give to anyone who wants to start working for themselves.

Two Musicians

I once worked at a place that had a recording studio. As a result, I met many young people who aspired to greatness in the field of popular music.

One young man talked a great deal about the musical masterpieces he wanted to create. The only thing holding him back, he said, was that someone needed to pay for him to have hundreds of hours in the studio, buy him some expensive instruments, hire a few session musicians to help out... and so on. He was frustrated that nobody was sufficiently impressed by his amazing creative talent (which he assured us he had) to pay for all this.

Another youngster who came to the studio told me his story. He had a rather different approach. Starting off with a cheap acoustic guitar, he went busking to earn a bit of money. He also performed a few shows in a bar near where he lived. It took a while but he eventually saved up enough money to buy a couple of days in our studio which he used to record a demo tape of his three or four best songs. He planned to sell copies of this tape at gigs to raise a bit of money and also send it to a few agents and producers.

I can't tell you for sure that the first guy never got anywhere while the second guy went on to enjoy an amazingly successful career. I can say, with certainty, that the second guy was going about things the right way and was far more likely to succeed.

Two Entrepreneurs

Here's another example.

I once knew someone who said he was going to set up a new business selling telephone equipment and services. He talked at great length about all the wonderful ideas he had and how much money he was going to make. To listen to him talk, you'd think he was going to usher in a new dawn of telephonic services, setting new standards and having his own statue in the Telephony Pioneers Hall Of Fame.

The only flaw in this beautiful vision was that he never actually got around to setting up the business. The problem, he explained, was that he needed a large amount of investment in order to rent some office space, hire some staff, buy some office equipment and pay all his up-front manufacturing and marketing costs. He felt rather disappointed that nobody seemed desperately keen to throw large chunks of cash at him to pay for all this.

Meanwhile, someone else I knew started up a business selling information booklets about various cities and tourist hotspots. His up-front investment was almost zero. To start, he wrote a guide about things to do in his home city of Oxford. He typed it up, pasted in some pictures and made fifty photocopies.

He went out on to the streets of Oxford and tried to sell his booklet to people. After some long days and sore feet, he eventually sold all fifty copies. This meant he had some money. He repeated this process until he had enough cash to invest in some equipment that enabled him to create better, more appealing booklets that were easier to sell.

In time, he was able to grow the business and produce a range of tourist guides and related publications for Oxford and a few other cities with a healthy tourist trade. As well as having the satisfaction of converting his idea into reality, he enjoyed himself, kept busy, learned a lot and made some money.

Always Try To DIY

Do as much as you can for yourself, rather than asking or relying on other people.

When you start working for yourself, you'll have a lot of things to do. You have to create products or services, see to your marketing, get a website, handle the accounts and so on.

There will be some things you can do for yourself. Good! By taking care of them yourself you'll save some time and money.

There will be some things you can't do for yourself because you lack the necessary knowledge, experience or skill. For these things, use other people. However, never take this option too quickly or too lightly. Get as far as you can on your own.

Bear in mind that as soon as you ask someone else to do something, you become reliant on that person. If they turn out to be slow and unresponsive, you've got problems. You have to weigh the potential benefit (getting the task done) against the potential downside. This isn't always an easy calculation. All you can do is trust to your best judgment under the circumstances.

In the fullness of time, you will be able to do less and delegate more. You will build up a network of people you know you can trust to take care of various tasks for you. However, in the early days, do as much as you can for yourself.

Delegation Difficulties

Delegation is a difficult subject for self-employed people. Unfortunately, it's one that is often discussed in rather glib terms that I think can be unhelpful and misleading.

Some people strongly recommend that you delegate as much as you can, as often as you can. The theory goes that by delegating a lot of mundane tasks, you free yourself to focus on the things you're good at and the areas of your business where you can deliver the most value. It's true, say the experts, that when you delegate you may have to accept a slight dip in performance. Nonetheless, it's a smart move and worth it in the long run.

This is all well and good but there is an equal and opposite theory. It can be argued that, given the time and effort needed to communicate with someone else and show them how to perform task X, it's easier and quicker to just do it yourself, even if it means you don't get to bed until 2am.

While this means a bit more work for you, it means you never have to contend with performance problems — such as discovering that the person you asked to help is about as much use as a salt shaker on the International Space Station and you end up doing all the work yourself anyway.

I don't think there's a simple, easy answer when it comes to delegation and I'm always rather wary of people who suggest there is. All you can do is see what works for you. If you can delegate various tasks in a way that makes a significant positive difference for you and your business, then by all means go right ahead. But if you can't, and the costs outweigh the benefits, it's just not worth it.

Business guru Tom Peters has a lot to say about this tricky subject in his excellent book 'In Search Of Excellence', which is well worth a look.

Delegation And Delay

There's one more thing to understand about delegation: other people always take longer than you would to get something done. The simple truth is that nobody is ever going to care about your work, plans and dreams as much as you do. Hence if there's a task that would take you a day, and you entrust it to someone else, don't be surprised if they take five days to get it done. This happens even when people work hard and have the best of intentions. You need to be aware of this whenever you delegate and factor it in to your schedule.

Connect To Effect: Email, Call, Meet

When I first started working for myself, I relied far too much on impersonal forms of contact such as writing a letter or sending an email. It took me a long time to realise the value and importance of actually meeting people and connecting with them.

It's not that I had anti-social tendencies. I just didn't appreciate that efficiency isn't everything and that personal connection makes a big difference (or at least it does to most people).

When it comes to selling, building your business, collaborating with people or doing deals, think in terms of imaginary pieces of gold. An email or any piece of written communication is worth one piece of gold to you. By all means use email and the written word but see it as a stepping stone to a phone call.

A phone call is worth ten pieces of gold to you. Now the other person can hear your tone of voice and how you express yourself. You can talk, interact and share a laugh. A phone call is great, but see it as a stepping stone to a meeting.

A meeting is worth a hundred pieces of gold to you. Now the other person can see you, shake hands, interact with you properly and share a coffee. What's more, all the 'non-verbal communication' stuff comes into play.

Of course, it's not always possible or desirable to go from email to phone call to meeting. There are always exceptions because there are exceptions to everything. Nonetheless it's generally a good idea, especially if you want to sell to people. You *can* sell by email and phone but it's a lot easier and more effective in person.

It's also a lot more fun. You should get into the habit of meeting people properly and enjoying the process of getting to know them and letting them get to know you. If you don't think you have very good 'people skills', you can probably find some other self-employed people who can help you in this area. Or, just keep meeting people until you become good at it! The best way to develop good people skills is to meet lots of people.

Meeting up with people in real life takes up a lot of time (far more than just sending an email or making a phone call). However, in the long run, I think it's a good policy. You are investing your time in the future success of your business.

This is one of many things I wish someone had told me a long time ago.

Living For Giving

Having mentioned the importance of connecting with people, I'd like to add the notion of 'living for giving'.

It's not necessarily a bad thing to think about what you can *get* from other people or what they can do for you. We all need help from time to time and it's nice to have a wide circle of friends and contacts whom you can call on when you need them.

However, think of this as the *end* point of your friendships and relationships rather than the *starting* point. Your starting point should be: what can you do for other people, how can you help them, what value can you add to their lives? Maybe you can give them your time, perform a small favour, offer a bit of insight and advice, put some work their way or at least recommend them to people. Perhaps you have some skill, talent or know-how that you can contribute to something you know they are working on.

If you have this outlook on life, and genuinely care about what you can do for others, you will end up with a good, strong social circle and plenty of friends who will help you when you need it. This is a very good position to be in and it makes your journey into self-employment a great deal easier than it would be otherwise.

In case this sounds a little too idealistic, let me add one point. It's true that some people will take from you and never give anything back. It's also true that some people will exploit your kindness and never repay it. Unfortunately, these things do happen from time to time and being taken for granted isn't any fun. All you can do is move on from such people and leave them be. Even if it's occasionally abused, 'living for giving' is still the best policy.

At an instinctive level, people can sense whether you are selfish or selfless, whether you're a taker or a giver, whether you're likely to do them a favour if they call on you. When people sense that you're a 'living for giving' sort of person, they instinctively warm to you. When they notice that you're often helping other people and doing favours, they are more likely to want to connect with you, work with you and include you in their projects.

Most of the self-employed people I know are definitely in the 'living for giving' category. They are constantly doing small favours for one another and thinking of ways in which they can be helpful. When I look back over the years, I can think of numerous times when self-employed friends have asked me for a favour or vice-versa. It's good to know that we're always ready and willing to help one another.

Talk And Listen

As you proceed along your self-employed journey, there are two things you can do that will greatly assist your chances of success. They are both easy and cost nothing yet a surprising number of people forget to do them:

- Talk to everyone.

- Listen to everyone.

Talk To Everyone

When you start your own business, talk to everyone you can about your ideas and plans. You never know when someone will just happen to mention something useful or helpful. When they do, take note of the opportunity and act on it promptly.

I am not saying you should *only* talk about your self-employment plans. By all means, talk about everything else under the sun. Just make sure that everyone you know is aware that you're planning to open a beauty salon; become an electrician; set up a dog walking service; develop a new range of healthy yoghurts and get them into supermarkets; make rocking horses for a living.

Make sure your family, relatives and friends all know about your plans and that all of *their* friends know as well. Get into the habit of mentioning it, in passing, at least once in every conversation. You can do this without being boring or tedious about it. This policy costs nothing and you never know when someone will give you some useful information, or a good lead, or become one of your customers.

Before I got my first job, I wasn't sure what I wanted to do. By common consent, I was largely unemployable. The only thing I seemed to be moderately good at was writing but I had no idea how to earn money doing it. I got chatting to a friend of mine about this. She said, "Oh, my brother works for a company that makes corporate videos. They sometimes use writers." That's how I got started.

Another good reason to talk to everyone about your plans is that it's a good way to find people who may want to collaborate with you, support you or give you some work. Most self-employed people have stories of random conversations that eventually led to great opportunities, fruitful collaboration or lucrative gigs.

Talk to everyone. Tell everyone your plans.

———————

Listen To Everyone

There's a good habit that I strongly recommend you develop: take a genuine interest in other people and listen to their story. Cultivate the art of active listening and really absorb what other people are saying and the way they talk about their life and experience.

I will make you three promises:

1. Everyone's story has at least one major surprise in it, something that you would never have guessed in a hundred years. Every life is a box of surprises.

2. Everyone's story has its hilarious chapters, very often in the form of experiences that were dark and difficult to live through at the time but which can be laughed at in retrospect.

3. Once in a while, just by listening to the people you meet, you will pick up wonderfully useful information that will make your life and your work ten times easier.

With regard to that third promise, let me share a quick story about a moment that changed my life.

Many years, when the internet was a *lot* younger than it is now, I was trying to set up my first e-commerce website. I had done some research and had a reasonably good idea of how such websites worked in theory. However, I had never created one and wasn't sure of the best way to go about it. I learned what I could, made several unsuccessful attempts, ran into problems, got a bit lost and tried again. In fact, I wrestled with this problem for five years. (I want to repeat that this was some years ago when there were fewer ready-made e-commerce solutions than there are now.)

One day I was meeting a client of mine called Tom. Our meeting had nothing to do with my e-commerce problem (in fact he was primarily interested in cold reading). However, during our conversation, while I was listening to Tom's story, I picked up on something that he mentioned in passing. To my great delight, I discovered that he knew all about the website problem I was trying to solve. In fact, he showed me how to solve it *in less than half an hour*. If I hadn't taken the time to listen to Tom, and made the effort to listen *well*, I might never have found the answer I was looking for.

I suggest you regard everyone you meet as a potential goldmine of insight, wisdom, great stories and useful information. That's *exactly* what they are.

Everyone Has Their Story

Let me add one more point about taking a genuine interest in everyone's story. Here's the way I look at it. Suppose you're in a maternity ward where there are several newborn babies lying in cots. At that stage, they're pretty much all alike with very little to distinguish them. They sleep, they make a noise when when they want to be fed or changed and that's about it.

Thirty years later... what a difference! Some are indoors types while others love nothing more than going for long, exhausting treks in the pouring rain. Some are academic high achievers while others have barely ever opened a book. Some are extroverts with a vast social network while others are generally quiet and prefer their own company. Some have extreme political views while others hardly ever think about politics. Some love refined classical music while others crave ear-splitting heavy metal bands, the louder the better. Some are very practical while others couldn't hammer a nail in straight.

Whenever I meet someone, I'm fascinated by the story that only they can tell: how they came to be who they are. I'm interested in both the nature and nurture factors. I want to know about the choices that were made for them and the ones they made for themselves. I think it's amazing that five more or less indistinguishable babies can grow up to become a geography teacher, a trapeze artist, an astrophysicist, a car mechanic and a jazz pianist.

I'm also fascinated by the fact that there are six billion people on the planet and no two are ever quite the same. Everyone has their unique story of forks in the road, options and choices, decisions and preferences that led to them being who they are. What's more, all of these stories are interesting and, in most cases, delightful to listen to.

The other great thing about listening to people is that you often gain some interesting perspectives. Some years ago, I was fortunate enough to visit the wonderful country of Indonesia. During my travels, I met a guide called Hari. He was intrigued by a few things he had heard about life in England. Among other things, he had heard that if English people want to eat fish, they go to a supermarket and buy some frozen fish sealed in a plastic packet inside a cardboard box — fish that might have been caught many weeks previously. Hari politely asked me if this was true. I said yes, this could happen.

Hari thought this was very sad and said he felt sorry for English people eating "old fish". He explained that when he wants fish for his family, he dives into the sea, catches a fish, takes it home and cooks it. "Fresh," he said, "much nicer!"

Yearn To Learn

When you work for yourself, it's a good policy to always keep an open mind and be willing to learn. In particular, I recommend you learn from at least three good sources:

- Learn from experience.

- Learn from teachers and trainers.

- Learn from other people.

Learn From Experience

First and foremost, learn from experience.

Experience is the only teacher you really need, the teacher you can always trust and the teacher that will never let you down. Experience is also the teacher that is available to everyone, all the time. Treasure experience. Chase it, cherish it, learn from it.

Of course, in order to gain experience you have to actually *do* something instead of just thinking or talking about it. If you spend three hours talking to a friend about the brilliant new business you're going to start up, or what a fantastic career you're going to have as a dancer, you won't have gained even a grain of experience so you won't have learned anything.

On the other hand, if you actually set up your business and get as far as making just one sale, or completing just one job, you will have gained valuable experience that's worth a month of just thinking and talking. The same is true if you complete even just a single paid gig as a model or comedian. No matter what the outcome, you will learn a great deal from the experience. Empty speculation tells you nothing and gets you nowhere. Experience is much more productive.

Let experience be your gold, your treasure, your valued teacher and the friend you always listen to. What's more, your experience will eventually be something valuable that other people, who want to learn from you, will be willing to pay for.

It's true that you can sometimes benefit from other people's experience, but it pays to be a little cautious. Remember that your life isn't their life, your circumstances are not their circumstances and your needs and preferences may not be the same. Your own experience is always the most valuable and useful teacher of all.

Learn From Teachers And Trainers

Wherever possible, be prepared to invest in your own education. Find the right teachers, trainers and courses for you and either develop your interests or gain new qualifications.

These days, 'Continuous Professional Development' or CPD is a very popular idea among many professionals, whether self-employed or not. I think it's an excellent concept. No matter what your area of special knowledge or expertise, there's always more for you to learn.

I should also mention that learning new things can be fun! For some self-employed people, CPD will mean working to obtain specific professional qualifications. For others, the precise nature of the CPD isn't all that important. It could involve learning a musical instrument, taking up yoga, going on a stand-up comedy course or attending the weekly meetings of your local photography club. All that matters is to keep learning and make sure you know more at the end of the year than you did at the start.

If you do want to study for specific qualifications, try to make sure they are valid qualifications that actually mean something — not just a piece of paper you get for turning up.

Investment in your education is investment in your future, which is precisely where you're going to live.

Learn From Other People

It pays to be attentive to other people and the way they do things. If you see that someone does something you do in a different way, find out about it — maybe their way is better. Some of the most productive conversations you can have with other self-employed people start with either, "How do you usually..." or "Do you know a better way to...".

Here's a very simple example.

I'm a writer by trade and by instinct, so in the past whenever I wanted to make a note of something I always used to write it down. Wherever I went, I always had a notebook with me for this purpose. In fact, I ended up with cupboard drawers full of small notepads.

I was slow to realise I could make notes using my phone's digital voice recorder. I noticed a friend do this one day and decided to try it. To my delight, I found it's much easier and more convenient! The notepads, alas, have been consigned to history and to the bin.

Know Your Tools

Whatever tools you use in your work, get to know them inside out. Learn how to use them properly and to best effect, and also learn how to maintain them.

If you use a computer a lot, learn everything there is to know about it and all the main pieces of software you use. Practise good 'housekeeping' of the machine itself and all your data.

If your work involves a sewing machine, camera or mixing desk, get to know every function it has and everything it can do. Devour the instruction manual, if there is one. Try things out, see what happens if you do this or that (without breaking anything).

Whenever you get a new bit of kit or hardware, see what every button, lever and dial does. Get curious and see if it can do things that aren't immediately obvious or that it's not supposed to be able to do. By doing this, you'll discover the full range of creative possibilities, some of which others will miss. You'll also be better able to cope when things go wrong or let you down.

On the subject of tools you use for work, spend as much money as you can safely afford on good quality tools and equipment. Always invest some time and effort to research the best possible option for the job. Good quality tools and props pay for themselves time and time again.

Build On Success

Let's assume you've been working for yourself for a while and you've enjoyed a bit of success.

Don't rest on your success. Carry on developing your art or your talent. Carry on creating and inventing. Carry on coming up with new ideas and ventures and things to try. Don't sit still just because you're in a good spot.

In the world of stand-up comedy, one of the first major aims of any aspiring star is to get to the point where they have twenty minutes of strong material (because this is how long an average spot in a comedy club lasts).

Many top comedians say that when you have twenty minutes of good material, the best thing you can do is ditch it, stop relying on it and start again. Go through the slow, arduous business of developing another twenty minutes of strong, usable material. When you've done that, stop using it and repeat the process a third time. Great! Now you've got an hour of strong material, meaning you do extended sets or a show at a major festival. This will help you to get noticed and be taken seriously as someone who has more than just a couple of good jokes to offer.

You might think this is obvious, common sense advice. However, there are comedians who develop their 'solid' twenty minutes and then more or less give up writing any new stuff — coasting along with the same material for as long as possible. The same thing happens in other areas of endeavour. People sometimes reach a certain level of achievement and for some reason 'switch off', content to stay where they are.

A good attitude is to see each achievement and piece of progress as a step to reach the next level, the next chapter in your story. You've come up with a hit product? Good! It will bring in some money. Use this to develop the next, even better product. You're getting a steady flow of bookings? Good! Get the evidence together (photos, video, testimonials) and use this as promotional ammunition to get even more bookings, or bigger and better ones.

You're doing some work for an impressive, big-name company? Good! Get the evidence and tell all the other impressive, big-name companies about it. Maybe they'll hire you too. Use each bit of success as a stepping stone to the next one. Your success story will have a hundred chapters in it. Don't stop turning the pages at the end of chapter seven.

Don't Be A Bond Villain

Having mentioned using each bit of success as a step to the next, I'm not saying this process has to go on forever. You don't have to decide that nothing short of complete global domination will do. You're not a villain in a James Bond film.

Like many things in life, this clearly comes down to a matter of balance. Lack of ambition is one mistake but too much ambition is another. If you don't think there's any such thing as 'too much ambition', try to take a running jump across the Grand Canyon and see if you end up looking heroic.

There comes a point where you can be happy with what you've achieved, you're doing all right financially and you realise you don't need to push yourself to the point where you burn out and even your best friends haven't seen you in months.

All I'm saying is that you shouldn't get off the success train too early. The next few stops might be the best ones.

To Get It Right, Get It Written

Whenever you're doing business with someone, get the practical details in writing: what you're agreeing to do, what you have said you'll supply, where you have agreed to be and at what time, how much time you've agreed to spend on something... and so on.

Details matter. Either ask the other person to put the details in writing so you can confirm them or do it yourself. This is a very good habit to get into: write down the details, share them with the other person and get their response or confirmation in writing. All that matters is that there's a written record somewhere that you can *both* refer back to.

This simple practice avoids all those conversations that begin with, "Oh, I thought you said..." / "I was told you said Thursday." / "What I thought you meant was... ."

Is it always possible or practical to get details in writing? No. Sometimes, this just isn't going to happen. Nonetheless, it *is* the best policy and helps you to avoid letting other people down. It also helps you to avoid those occasions when other people let *you* down.

Put all the relevant details in writing. Circulate them to all concerned. Get responses and confirmation. Have a record you can refer back to if any dispute arises.

* * *

What's Next

The next section is about good values to have plus the highly illuminating parable of Sleazy and Sunny.

12. Good Values To Have

"A person who won't read has no advantage over one who can't read."

— Mark Twain

12. Good Values To Have

Your values define who you are, how you behave and what you expect of yourself and others. To a large extent, your values also determine how likely you are to succeed. Just as strong trees don't grow from weak roots, success tends not to follow from poor values and low standards of behaviour. Here are some good values to have when you start working for yourself.

Be Reliable

These are the two words I suggest you carve into the side of a nearby mountain so you can contemplate them every morning, by the light of the sunrise, and let them guide your day, your heart and your life. Let them be your mantra, your code, the signature of your spirit and the hallmark of your work.

You want to work for yourself, make money and fulfil your potential? Great! The single biggest favour you can do for yourself, and for everyone you ever deal with, is this: be a reliable person.

If you say you're going to do something, do it.

If you say you're *not* going to do something, *don't* do it.

If you give a commitment to anyone, don't let them down.

If you've said you'll get back to someone, don't leave them chasing you or wondering why you didn't do what you said you were going to do.

If you've said you're going to be somewhere at a given time, be there! Plan ahead and allow some contingency time. Getting somewhere a bit early is never a problem. Getting somewhere a bit late is often a problem and is also inconsiderate.

Check details, so you don't accidentally go to the wrong place. Get all the relevant details in writing. Written information has a beautiful clarity that you can't get from a garbled message over the phone or a half-remembered snippet of conversation.

Being reliable is one of the rarest of all human traits. It's a wonderful way to differentiate yourself from other people and to succeed where others fail. Organise your time, your day, your efforts and your logistics so that you are a reliable person rather than a time-waster. Everyone you deal with will appreciate the effort you make to be reliable.

Don't spend your life apologising. "I'm sorry, I forgot." "I'm sorry, I wrote the address down wrong." "I'm sorry, my alarm clock didn't go off and then the traffic was really bad." Anyone can go through life saying sorry. It requires precisely zero excellence to do this.

Get a house brick and write, "I'm sorry" on it. If you go through life apologising to people all the time, then this dumb, lifeless house brick can do everything you can do. Imagine that: you can't perform any better than a brick. It's better to organise your life so that you never have anything to apologise for.

Of course, life isn't perfect. Things can go wrong. There are days when the transport network becomes a 'transport not work'. Sometimes, you can't avoid arriving late. Nobody has the key to perfection. What matters is your *intent*, how hard you try to be reliable and how conscientious you are about it. It doesn't take long to get a reputation for reliability or a *lack* of reliability. If you get a reputation for being unreliable, you will find it very hard to be successful. People will tend to feel, quite rightly, that dealing with you is such hard work that it's just not worth it.

If you can't be reliable, you can't be anything.

Don't Over-Commit

When it comes to being reliable, here's a bit of advice: don't over-commit yourself.

If two people in different places both say they want to see you at 3 pm on Tuesday, don't say yes to them both. Unless you have mastered the art of being in two places at once, you are going to let down at least one of these people, which is annoying.

If you promise Jack that you'll get task A done this week, and it's going to take you roughly all week to do it, don't also promise Jill that you'll get task B done in the same time. You are going to let down either one or the other, or both.

You may think this is so obvious as to not be worth stating. Many years ago, I would have agreed with you. Alas, my experience of life and of people suggests that this is, in fact, not as obvious as it should be. There are many people who are so determined to please everyone, all the time, that they make the mistake of over-committing. As a result, they let people down and get a reputation for not being very reliable.

Good intentions are fine. Over-committing yourself is pointless and gives people the impression that trying to work with you is hopeless.

Be Honourable

Working for yourself will be a lot easier if you build a reputation for fair, decent, honest behaviour. If you get a name for dishonest dealing, it will take you a long time to shake it off.

Just because some people trade dishonestly doesn't mean you have to. Lick your wounds, move on, laugh and learn. Be glad you don't have their mentality or their life.

Admit Your Mistakes

Another part of being fair and honourable is this: when you make a mistake, admit it. Don't pretend that you're perfect. If you make a mistake, you might lose a little bit of respect. If you make a mistake and then make excuses or try to blame someone else, as if you're the world's only consistently flawless human being, you will lose a lot of respect.

If you are honest about your faults and mistakes, you'll find that most other self-employed people respect you for this and also tend to be very understanding and forgiving.

Sleazy And Sunny

Here's a true story. There was once a magician who always had plenty of work and liked helping other performers. Let's call him Sunny. There was another magician who wanted to get more work. We'll call him Sleazy. One time, Sunny decided to help Sleazy and gave him a well-paid gig. The client would pay Sunny, he would take his commission and then pay the rest to Sleazy.

When he was at the gig, Sleazy took the client to one side and said, "I don't know what you've paid Sunny to hire me but in future if you come to me directly, I'll give you a better price." Sleazy was trying to cut Sunny out of the picture, even though Sunny had just done him a favour.

The client immediately called Sunny on the phone and explained what Sleazy had just done. "You know that magician you sent here? He's just tried to cut you out of any future deals."

Obviously, Sunny never gave Sleazy any more work. What's more, it wasn't long before everyone in the magic world knew the story, so nobody else was very keen to give Sleazy any work either. Why would they? They all knew he had behaved in a treacherous, disloyal, greedy and ungrateful way.

112

Do The Right Thing

Mark McCormack was a legendary US sports agent whom many say created the modern 'celebrity endorsement' industry. He founded IMG, one of the greatest agencies of its kind.

Mark often told a story about one of his clients, a famous golfer. One time, this golfer happened to get some 'appearance' engagements that, as it happened, did not come through IMG. The golfer could have quietly pocketed the fees he got and IMG would never have known. Instead, he sent IMG the percentage they would normally have taken as commission. Why? Because the golfer knew that IMG had worked hard to raise his celebrity profile. These engagements probably wouldn't have arisen if not for the reputation that McCormack had helped to build. In short, the golfer just thought it was the right thing to do.

I suggest you follow this example. Always do the right thing. In particular, do the right thing when you're dealing with other self-employed people. We should all help one another, not stab one another in the back.

I believe that being honourable has a lot to do with success. If you're fair and honest with everyone, it's easier to be successful. If you're not, it soon becomes almost impossible to succeed. Word gets round fast, and if you get known for being unfair or dishonest nobody wants to have anything to do with you.

I've made a lot of mistakes in my life. I'm not particularly smart or wise. However, I do know that I've always dealt with everyone fairly and honestly. Nobody has any grievances against me. If I can't be proud of much else, I can at least be proud of this.

Be Polite

Be a polite person. Say 'please' when you ask. Say 'thank you' when you receive. This is another remarkably easy way to differentiate yourself from other people and to do yourself a big favour when it comes to your success.

Having good manners does not, in itself, get you very far. The point is that having *bad* manners can very easily make people turn away from you.

If someone helps you or does you a favour, and you can't even be bothered to say 'thank you', you can't be surprised if they don't help you next time. You could easily end up with a reputation for being unappreciative of other people's time, effort and generosity.

Be Grateful

When you start working for yourself, some people will show you great kindness. Don't just take this for granted. Try to echo it and to show your appreciation.

Buy them a coffee. Buy them a drink. Do something that expresses and conveys your gratitude. Send them a little gift to say thank you. It's never been easier, quicker or cheaper to send someone a card, flowers, a book or a small gift to serve as a token of your gratitude. You can go online and make it happen in less than five minutes.

Kind people are extremely important and valuable in your life. Let them know you appreciate their kindness. Let me add two notes about this:

> 1. Be ready to accept that some people genuinely don't want anything in return.

> 2. You may want to check with the intended recipient of your kindness before you send them something they don't want. It's a shame when good intentions end up as unwanted gifts. You might feel sure a clockwork parrot that sings a variety of jazz standards is the cutest gift in the world but others might not share your tastes.

The Attitude Of Gratitude

It's a good idea to cultivate an 'attitude of gratitude'. It gives you a good perspective on any problems you may have.

Yes, it's annoying when someone promises they'll help me and then fails to do so. On the other hand, I've got clean, fresh drinking water available on tap, whenever I want it.

Yes, it's unfortunate when I desperately need to get somewhere and the train is delayed or cancelled. On the other hand, I've got lots of wonderful friends with amazing talents that never fail to impress and delight me.

Yes, I get frustrated if my car breaks down on a cold, wet night when I'm a long way from anywhere. On the more positive side, I've seen the view from the very top of the Petronas Towers and seen Frank Sinatra sing at the Royal Albert Hall.

Feel gratitude for the good and happy aspects of your life. Don't forget them, don't take them for granted.

Be Likeable (Rather Than Nice)

There's a difference between being nice and being likeable. Someone trying to be nice can all too often come across as suffering from low self-esteem. It's as if they're saying, in a rather simpering way, "I want to please you so much that you'll like me and be my friend."

I think a slightly better focus is to be likeable.

These aren't mutually exclusive traits — it's possible to be both. Just don't get caught in the trap of thinking that you can be so nice to someone, so often, that you can make them like you. This isn't how people and relationships work.

One of the most talented singers, musicians and songwriters I know is Kirsty Doody (née Newton). She can play just about every song you've ever heard of on almost any instrument (although she mainly plays piano and bass guitar). She also happens to be brilliantly funny.

There are many reasons why Kirsty enjoys a highly successful career as a teacher, musician and performer. She is certainly breathtakingly talented. However, she is also incredibly likeable. Nobody has a bad word to say about her and other performers love working with her on shows and recordings. Follow Kirsty's example. Be likeable.

If you want to be more likeable, try reading Nicholas Boothman's book, 'How to make people like you in 90 seconds or less'. Just don't make the mistake of thinking that buying the book will, in itself, make any difference. You have to study it, understand the various techniques that Boothman describes and use them in real life.

Under-promise, Over-deliver

Always try to exceed people's expectations.

When people get less than they were expecting from you, nobody's happy and your reputation suffers. When people get more than they were expecting, everybody's happy and your reputation grows.

It's not just a case of supplying a little extra product or giving a bit more time than it says on the contract. See if you can provide extra value, or be more thorough and thoughtful than other people in your line of work. Pay attention to small details that can make a big difference to how satisfied your customers feel. Let clients see that you care about giving as much value as you can and exceeding their expectations. This is a great way to build a positive word-of-mouth reputation.

Have A Sense Of Humour

If you're going to work for yourself, I think it's important to arm yourself with a robust and fully functioning sense of humour. Believe me, there will be many occasions when you'll need it.

A good sense of humour can be your ballast, your shield, your raincoat, your parachute and your personal life support unit. Your journey into the world of self-employment doesn't come with many guarantees but here's one: you will often be tested on your ability to laugh in the face of misfortune. I suggest you strive to be impressively good at this. Your sanity may depend on it.

Someone once said that life will either make you laugh or make you cry. If this is the only choice, then I choose to laugh. A sense of humour and a love of laughter will make your journey a lot easier. Remember, 'A smile is the shortest distance between two people.'

The Two Actors

I once met up with a friend who is an actor. The day before, he had auditioned for a role in a major TV show. He was perfect for this role and had prepared very diligently for the audition. It was the kind of role that would make a huge difference to his career: fame, fortune and, in all probability, a lot more work.

He didn't get the part. What's worse, they didn't even give him a chance. The people conducting the audition barely paid him any attention. When I met up with him, my friend looked despondent and defeated. He said that nobody was ever going to give him a break. Staring into the bottom of his coffee cup, he talked in flat, lifeless tones about giving up. "I realise now that I'm just kidding myself," he said. "I'm never going to get anywhere."

As it happens, about a month later I met up with another friend of mine, also an actor, who had been through a similar experience: big role, high hopes, flat rejection, barely even given a chance.

As she told me about this disastrous audition, she was full of smiles, laughter and jokes. She turned the tale into a wickedly funny anecdote, acting the whole thing out and portraying the stark contrast between her high hopes and the rather dismal reality of 'The Audition From Hell'. As my friend told her story, she was full of energy and zest for life. The experience clearly hadn't made one jot of difference to her confidence. To her, it was just a great story to share of how things can sometimes go spectacularly wrong.

We're not all made the same way. Some of us are naturally funnier than others. Some of us are loud and lively, others more quiet and thoughtful. Nonetheless, if you're going to work for yourself, you'll find it very useful to have a healthy sense of humour. Be ready to laugh at the iniquities of life and then wake up the next day ready to try all over again.

The best definition of humour I know of comes from the genius James Thurber. He wrote, "Humour is emotional turbulence recalled in tranquillity." Isn't that beautiful?

When life doesn't go your way, enjoy it. Laugh, learn a lesson or two, move on. A disappointing experience doesn't have to be a heavy chain you carry round with you. It can just be a brilliant story you share with friends and then forget about.

* * *

What's Next?

Working for yourself is never going to be seamless bliss. What should you do if people let you down, treat you badly or don't believe in you and your ideas? The next section is about good ways to respond to these and other problems.

13. Good Ways To Respond

"Would you like me to give you a formula for success? It's quite simple, really. Double your rate of failure. You are thinking of failure as the enemy of success. But it isn't at all. You can be discouraged by failure or you can learn from it. So go ahead and make mistakes. Make all you can. Because remember that's where you will find success."

— Thomas J. Watson

13. Good Ways To Respond

Your experience of working for yourself is unlikely to consist of open roads and clear skies all the way. You will experience bumps, clouds, storms, frustrations and disappointments. There will occasionally be grit in your shoe, splinters in your fingers and bruises with a story attached. This is your destiny.

You can't choose whether or not bad news comes along. You *can* choose how you respond to it. Here are some good suggestions.

When People Let You Down

There are times when people annoy you by being hopeless and incompetent. They forget details, fail to turn up, give you the wrong information, waste your time, don't return messages, seem hopelessly disorganised and terrible at their job.

Whenever you encounter this phenomenon, rejoice! Why? Because all these incidents remind you how *easy* it is to be better than average and more successful than most people.

Imagine what it would be like to live in a society where everyone was impressively brilliant, reliable and efficient all the time. They never put a foot wrong and always delivered great results. It would be pretty tough to compete and be successful, wouldn't it?

But you don't live in a society like that. Incompetence is all around you, all the time. So rejoice and celebrate!

When People Treat You Badly

It can be very hard to accept, but nobody actually *intends* to treat you badly. It's not as if they woke up one morning and thought, "I know, today I will treat so-and-so badly." It might *feel* that way but it's not how people work.

When you're born, you get dealt a hand of cards. You spend the rest of your life playing them as best you can, striving to be happy, content and fulfilled. This is what everyone is doing, all the time.

When someone seems to treat you badly, be understanding. They're just trying to play their cards and muddle through life as best they know how. Just like you, me and everyone else.

You don't know their story or their situation. You don't know their pain or problems, past or present. Maybe they've had a much rougher ride than you. Be forgiving. Someone once said that when you forgive someone, it's like releasing a prisoner except the prisoner is you, yourself.

Forgiving doesn't have to mean that you forget. Forgiving means you neither harbour any grudge nor carry any hate forward with you. You may decide, however, that it's best if you and the other person gently drift in separate directions.

Never carry any hate or anger around with you. They are both heavy rocks on your back that slow you down and gradually wear you out. Neither hate nor anger can ever help you to achieve anything so leave them out of the equation.

Count To Ten!

My friend Kathleen Hawkins (author and professional speaker) offers some excellent advice about counting to ten.

She says that part of being self-confident and successful means you stand up for your rights, hold people accountable for their behaviour and give them a chance to redeem themselves if necessary. However, you first of all have to get your ego out of the way. A 'knee-jerk' response isn't going to help.

As soon as you feel that someone has done you wrong (in your opinion), take a deep breath and count to ten. This could be ten minutes, ten hours or ten days — however long it takes you to cool down.

During this time, you might want to go for a walk or a run, get some exercise or discuss the problem with someone who can help you to keep things in perspective.

When you get your ego out of the way and act rationally, without anger or feelings of revenge, you'll be coming from a position of strength. You'll think more clearly and, in a calm, positive frame of mind, be able to protect your interests, hold people responsible for their behaviour and give them an opportunity to correct the situation. You'll also give yourself a much better chance to evaluate what went wrong and guard against it happening again.

Kathleen has a much more good advice to offer. If you're serious about being successfully self-employed, I highly recommend that you read her excellent book 'Spirit Incorporated', which you'll find stimulating and eye-opening on many levels.

When People Don't Believe In You

When people don't believe in you and say they don't think you're very good, rejoice! Why? Because it means you are on exactly the same path as anyone who has ever enjoyed any success!

Think of anyone you regard as successful in any field: business, entertainment, science, technology or whatever. I guarantee they went through exactly the same experience of being ignored and told they'll never get anywhere. So if you have this kind of experience, you're on the same path as every successful person in history!

When youngsters come on to the job market, many of them end up making the same complaint: "Everyone says they won't hire me until I have gained some experience but how can I get experience if nobody will hire me?"

It's the same when you're trying to be successful. Before you're a success, nobody (or hardly anyone) believes in you or wants to be your friend. After you're a success, everyone believes in you and wants to be your friend. Before, the media will ignore you and swat you away like a fly. After, they'll offer you all the interviews and coverage you want because they can make money out of you.

In the early days of your self-employed journey, you will have setbacks and disappointments. You will meet condescending people who are very dismissive of you and your efforts. You will face unfair criticism. There's a very good reply to all these kinds of experiences: have a brilliantly successful life.

I learned a lot about this from my friend Eddie Izzard, whom I met at university many years ago. We used to write and perform comedy sketch shows together. Eddie went through ten years of 'experts' telling him he had no talent and no future in comedy. He decided to carry on and have a successful career anyway. These days, he's an internationally successful comedian who can fill major venues all over the world. The DVDs of his shows have all been best-sellers. He also has a successful career as an actor in live theatre, movies and TV. He has success, wealth and a very comfortable lifestyle.

Where are all those 'experts' now? Where are all the brilliant minds who dismissed Eddie, had no time for him, rejected him and told him that he didn't have what it took to be successful? They are gone, silent, nowhere to be found.

Eddie wasn't bothered that they didn't believe in him. He didn't need them to. He believed in himself.

The Curse Of Unusual Dreams

At the start of this book, I added a note for younger readers saying it's all right to have unusual ambitions. Not everyone wants to be a teacher or perform an administrative role in local government. Dreams can take many shapes, hearts can be called from many directions. Some people want to be a contortionist or become a master puppeteer.

The fact that it's all right, and indeed admirable, to have unconventional ambitions cannot be stated too often or too loudly, given that the opposing view enjoys such widespread currency. The world is rarely short of loud voices sneering at unconventional ambitions. This is the curse of unusual dreams.

It starts with the kind of misguided 'advice' that just assumes one kind of ambition is more worthwhile than another, as if wanting to work in an office is intrinsically better than wanting to be a ventriloquist. It continues throughout adult life, with people thinking it's perfectly okay to make snide comments about unusual aspirations. She works in a circus? What a shame. Couldn't she get a *proper* job?

This kind of flabby, sneering prejudice gets institutionalised in countless ways. Go to any official source of careers advice. You want a career in banking or construction? Terrific, here's a stack of information. Want to be an actor, sword-swallower or illusionist? You're on your own.

These palaces of official wisdom may claim they must cater primarily to people seeking 'normal' careers, given that they are in the majority. I say they are *causing* the bias as much as they are reflecting it. If you only provide one door, you can't justify this by saying it's the one most people use. This type of sly and covertly toxic 'reasoning' has been used throughout history to disguise arbitrary prejudice as respectable policy. At one time, women couldn't study to become surgeons. Why not? "Because women don't want to be surgeons and have no aptitude for the job." How do you know? "Look around, how many female surgeons do you see? None! That proves it!"

It's going to be a while, I suspect, before the young person who wants to be a fire-eater or mime artist is offered the same respect and guidance as a budding accountant. In the meantime, all we can do, as self-employed people including performers, artists and entertainers, is stand together, look after our own and share the joy of our vocations.

"And those who were seen dancing were thought to be insane
by those who could not hear the music."
— Nietsche

When People Aren't Buying

There will be times in your career when you're selling but nobody seems to be buying. It happens.

When you're trying to sell something, and you get one 'no sale' after another, rejoice! Why? Because it means you're getting closer to a 'yes'.

Here's a story that features in textbooks about selling. A man had a young son who wanted to earn some pocket money during the school holidays. The man said, "Do what I did when I was your age. Go round door to door and offer to do gardening chores for people — say you'll mow their lawn or trim their hedges for a small fee."

The son went out to try. He returned several hours later, dejected. He said, "I can't believe it! I knocked on about thirty doors and only one person gave me any work and some money! Just one! Everyone else said no. I feel so defeated."

The father said, "Look at it a different way. Suppose you know for sure that you're going to get one sale in every thirty attempts. When you get turned down the first time, great! You're making progress towards your next sale which is now just 29 knocks away. When you get the second refusal, even better — now your next sale is just 28 knocks away. Of course, it won't work out *precisely* like that. You may get a few sales close together, then some longer gaps. But it will average out."

His son now had a much more positive attitude. He didn't mind each time he got turned down. He just moved on to the next house, knowing he was getting closer to a 'yes'. He enjoyed doing the work and made a fair bit of money.

This isn't just a cute story from sales textbooks. It works in real life. In the past, I've managed sales and marketing teams for some large companies. I always made sure the sales people understood that every 'no' is just the prelude to a 'yes'. Persistence is the key to many locks.

Of course, it would be overly simplistic to suggest that if you aren't getting any sales, the answer is always a matter of persistence. There are as many other possibilities as there are pages in a manual about selling. Low sales might be the warning light that tells you the product isn't right, you haven't found the right market or you're not selling in the right way. I'm well aware of these and other possibilities.

In this section, I just wanted to point out an unsuccessful sales pitch isn't always and automatically a reason to panic. Maybe you're just one more knock away from a successful sale.

When Plans Go Wrong

Imagine yourself standing amid the wrecked and smouldering ruins of your once proud and beautiful plans, surveying the landscape as you shake your head in sorry disbelief and realise there's nothing you can salvage from the scene. You worked hard to create something wonderful. Now, there's nothing but smoke, ruins and shrapnel beneath grey, drizzling skies of humiliation.

If you choose to work for yourself, there will be times like these. You can trust me on this. How should you respond?

You have several options. For example, you can go into a fierce sulk and feel sorry for yourself. You can also blame other people and despair at being surrounded by idiots on all sides. Alternatively, you can blame yourself and see how much damage you can do to your self-esteem.

I'd like to suggest a different option.

Have a good think about what happened. Ask yourself a few questions to see what, if anything, you can learn from the experience. What could you have done differently, or better? Could you perhaps have thought ahead and anticipated possible problems? Could you have handled the situation better, more calmly or more successfully? Then, forget about it and move on.

This is a good option for all sorts of reasons. For one thing, you get into the habit of taking responsibility for yourself and your own actions. This is much better than externalising the problem: pretending everything that goes wrong is always someone else's fault.

Secondly, it means you spend a lot less time feeling sorry for yourself (which is boring for you) or moaning (which is boring for everyone else).

Thirdly, you're more likely to learn from the experience so you're less likely to get things wrong in future. Learning is a really good idea, unless you want to go through life only equipped with whatever insight and wisdom you had when you were five.

There are times when you may want to feel a bit sorry for yourself. It's human nature. But a little is enough. I think a good natural cut off point is your next night's sleep. Sit around and feel in a bad mood if you want, but once you go to sleep, that's it! When you wake up, you're refreshed and facing a bright new day full of great possibilities. Leave yesterday's emotional baggage behind.

No-one can change the past. No-one can stop you changing the future.

Consider All The Possibilities

Still on the subject of things going wrong, let me add one further point. Whenever things don't turn out the way you hoped, remind yourself that you can never be certain what would have happened.

Suppose you pay a sales visit to a big, important company, Whizzo, and hope to win a big contract with them. You try your best but, alas, the Whizzo people don't buy. No sale, no deal.

This might feel very disappointing but it's worth keeping an open mind. It's possible you could have got the deal only to find that Whizzo are a terrible company to deal with, make excessive demands, keep trying to change the terms of the deal, don't keep to their side of the agreement and take ages to pay you. In other words, they're a total nightmare and, quite honestly, not worth the trouble.

In life, getting what you think you want doesn't always turn out well. Sometimes, *not* getting what you want works out better in the long run. It's natural to form expectations and hope that things will turn out a certain way. Just remember that countless 'disappointments' lead to wonderful chapters in life.

When An Idea Doesn't Work

When you try an idea and it doesn't work, rejoice! Why? Because you're learning and discovering what *does* work, based on experience. This is a good thing.

Think for a moment of every significant advance in human civilisation: the wheel, writing, irrigation, arable farming and crop rotation, moveable type, steam power, refrigeration, electricity, radio waves, powered flight, rock music, the microchip, the internet, the clip-on bow tie and the ability to print photos on to cakes. A remarkable track record of magnificent achievements.

Do you know how we, as a species, managed to take all these great steps forward? By people trying things, ditching the ideas that don't work and refining the ones that do. This is what we've done, over and over again, for thousands of years.

Every time you try an idea that doesn't work, don't worry. Remind yourself that you're in very good company. You're having precisely the same experience as anyone who ever invented anything great or useful. Stand up straight and take your place among this historic pantheon of greatness with pride.

126

When You've Got A Problem

When you've got a problem to deal with, rejoice! Why? Because it's a chance to show how brilliant you are at solving problems. A chance to shine, to win, to triumph!

Imagine for a moment that you're a highly talented pianist. You love playing and everyone who hears you is impressed and delighted. Now imagine that you're never near a piano and therefore never get a chance to show what beautiful music you can create. You would feel a bit frustrated, wouldn't you? How annoying it would be to have this ability, this talent, but never any opportunity to demonstrate it.

It would be the same if you never had a problem to deal with. Between your ears you have a human brain. This is the most complex, most wonderful thing that we currently know of, in the entire universe. It is also formidably good at solving problems.

Among other things, the human brain has figured out how to split the atom, send videos across the internet, paint the Sistine Chapel ceiling, perform open heart surgery, play chess to grandmaster level, defeat smallpox, build an electron microscope, cultivate orchids and design a rocket that can fly to the moon. You have the same raw material, the same basic stuff between your ears, as the people who achieved all these things and solved all these problems. Enjoy your opportunity to show how superb you are at solving problems.

(I said that the human brain is the most wonderful thing that we currently know of. As the comedian Emo Philips pointed out, the thing telling us that the human brain is so wonderful is, of course, the human brain. So it's possible the verdict is a bit biased.)

Problems To Solutions: The 'Therefore' Link

Whenever you mention a problem or something that's blocking your progress, try this trick: see the statement of the problem as the first part of a statement about the solution. Try a 'therefore' link and see where it takes you.

Here's an example of what I mean. Don't just say, "I don't know how to set up a website." Continue the thought: "...*therefore* I either need to learn how to do this or find someone to do it for me. Who can I ask about this? Where can I get some good information? Who do I know that has already dealt with this problem — they would probably be good to talk to."

Don't just say, "I need a video camera for this but I don't have one."
Continue the thought and the sentence: "...*therefore* I'm going to think
how I can buy one, borrow one, hire one or find someone who has one
who can help me."

If you only say the first part, "I don't know how to do that", you're just
stating your current limitations. If you dwell on this thought you're just
wasting time. If, instead, you try a 'therefore' link, it might lead to some
positive ideas about the next steps to take.

In short: spend less time talking about the problem and more time talking
about what you can do to solve it.

If you can take some steps to fix the situation, good. What if you can't?
Well, it's very rare for there to be absolutely *no* positive steps you can
take. However, if this is the case, then you've discovered something not
to waste any of your time on. You're free to get on with something else!

* * *

What's Next?

When you're trying to run your own business, some things are best
avoided. In the next chapter, we're going to look at a few of them,
including Granite Trampolines and Time Vampires!

14. Things To Avoid

"It's never too late to have a happy childhood."

— Berkeley Breathed

14. Things To Avoid

There's much to look forward to when you work for yourself: good times, success, financial rewards, the joy of a job well done. However, there are also a few common problems worth trying to avoid. Let's take a look at a few of them.

Avoid Atrocious Advice

When you start working for yourself, you'll meet many people offering wisdom and advice. Of course, this can be very useful. The problem is that a lot of 'advice' is misleading, inaccurate or just plain wrong. How can you spot bad, useless advice? Here are some tests to apply.

1. A Sales Pitch Is Not Advice

Is the person giving 'advice' really just trying to sell you something? If so, they are not worth listening to. There's nothing wrong with people trying to sell you things. However, if someone *pretends* to be innocently offering advice when in fact they want to sell you something, it's a good idea to walk away.

If you suspect you're on the receiving end of a sales pitch dressed up as impartial advice, simply ask the direct question, "At the end of this, are you going to try to sell me something?"

Learning to ask this question at an early stage in the proceedings can save you a lot of time.

2. An Opinion Is Not A Fact

Sometimes people offer advice with a great air of authority, as if they're sharing tremendous insight and wisdom. Everything about their tone conveys a profound sense of reliable expertise.

Genuine expertise can be very helpful, but in many cases the 'expert' is simply expressing an *opinion*, no more and no less. There's nothing wrong with this, but you could ask a hundred smart people for their opinion about something and get a hundred different answers.

If you're trying to make good decisions, always prefer facts to opinions. The difference is that you can't check an opinion but you *can* check facts. You can do research and see what the data actually tells you.

3. Glib Comments Are Not Solutions

Some people like to address complex problems in rather glib and simplistic terms: "You need a new computer? No problem. I know a guy in the trade. He can get top quality stuff dead cheap. Easy! He sorted me out a while back. I'll get his number for you."

People who say things like this may be full of good intentions. If they have quite an affable, cheery manner, their 'solution' to the problem you're discussing might sound fairly plausible. After all, wouldn't it be nice if tough problems had quick, simple solutions?

Unfortunately, a glib attitude rarely delivers good answers. For example, different people may have radically different requirements when they're choosing a computer. A machine that would be ideal for one person might be a very poor choice for someone else. Just because Jack is very happy with his 'cheap' computer doesn't mean it's the right choice for Jill. It's like suggesting everyone takes the same size shoes.

If someone suggests a problem has a glib, easy solution, be cautious. Perhaps they simply don't, or can't, appreciate fine details and subtle distinctions.

4. Beware Survivorship Bias

Sometimes people give advice based on their own life and experience. This is all very well, but if their own success was a complete fluke then their advice isn't going to be worth very much to you. This is known as 'survivorship bias' and it crops up with remarkable frequency, particularly when people are dispensing life advice.

Suppose a thousand people take part in a lottery and one of them wins the big main prize. Would you go and ask that person for their advice and insights about how to choose lottery numbers? Of course not — there's nothing they can tell you because it was a fluke result. However, many people who got very lucky in life like to think they are in a position to pass on wisdom and advice.

Be aware of Survivorship Bias and always bear in mind that the 'wisdom' you're hearing might be coming from someone no smarter than a lottery winner. They can be forgiven for thinking they have actually *achieved* something (as opposed to just being lucky). This is only human nature. However, you don't need to succumb to the same delusion.

Randall Munroe writes and draws a wonderful online comic series called XKCD. If you search for the single panel XKCD cartoon called 'Survivorship Bias', you will see this idea beautifully illustrated.

Avoid Granite Trampolines

From time to time as you build your career, you'll come across people who volunteer to help you, free of charge, for one reason or another. Free help sounds great, of course, but it pays to be cautious. Sometimes, the person volunteering to help, though full of good intentions, turns out to be as much use as a granite trampoline.

A few years ago, someone volunteered to help me with my online marketing. He was sure he could help me to make more money and I have no doubt he had sincere intentions. Nine months later, I was still waiting for *any* sign of progress. He literally hadn't even started. I realised nothing was going to happen and politely told him I would pursue other options.

During this time, I didn't try any new marketing initiatives of my own as I had assumed this helpful volunteer was going to open the door to greater success. In effect, I lost about nine months of potential business development.

If you meet someone like this, get all the arrangements in writing and agree a timescale. If they go 10% beyond the agreed timescale, this is acceptable. After all, life is uncertain and not everything runs smoothly to plan. Beyond that, pull the plug. You're not dealing with someone you can rely on.

This can get difficult because of the 'Bus Stop Problem'. The more time you've invested in waiting for a bus, the more you feel inclined to persist and see it through — because otherwise you'll waste the time you've already spent waiting. Also, the longer you have waited, the more likely it is that the bus must arrive soon. Alas, in life there are many buses that never come at all, so to speak.

All you can do is judge each case on its merits. If someone keeps promising and doesn't deliver, heed the warning signs and be prepared to walk away lest they waste your time forever.

Once in a while (to continue the metaphor), maybe you'll walk away and then see the bus turned up a minute later. Don't feel foolish. It was still the right decision based on past experience and the evidence you had at the time. It's one fluke among the ninety-nine times when walking away was the right thing to do because the bus never turned up.

What I have described as the 'Bus Stop Problem' is what psychologists refer to as the 'Sunk Cost Fallacy'. It's a fascinating phenomenon that affects everyone from gamblers to stock market investors. You may want to read about it.

Avoid Time Vampires

An important part of fulfilling your own potential is being willing to help others do the same. You'll often find that when you help others, you also help yourself. This is the theme of some of my favourite quotations, such as:

> "A bit of fragrance always clings to the hand that gives the rose."
> — Chinese proverb

However, having a kind and helpful attitude can lead to problems, as the following tale makes clear.

My friend Drew McAdam (mindreader and writer) was once a very successful writer of short stories. As well as being good at writing stories, he was also good at selling them and making money. His fame spread among people who like writing stories. Before long he was receiving lots of requests for help. People used to contact him and say, "Please give me tips and advice about writing stories and selling them."

Drew is, by nature, a very helpful sort of person. This being so, he spent many hours replying to these people and sharing his knowledge. This started to take up quite a lot of his time. He eventually devised a very smart policy. Whenever people contacted him for help, he said, "I will share everything I know and help you all I can. First of all, just go away and write me a story. It doesn't have to be any good. Just write me a story and then come back to me."

99% of these people never came back to him.

If people come to you for help that is going to take up a significant amount of your time, follow a simple plan: make it as time-consuming to ask for help as it will be to provide it. By asking the other person to do some work (such as writing a story in this example) you are filtering out those who want help without effort. It means that when you *do* spend some time trying to help people, you are helping the ones who will appreciate it and, in all probability, make the best use of whatever help and advice you can offer.

To put this another way, respect actions rather than words. Anyone can say, "I really want to learn". Words are easy and cheap. Actions count for a lot more. They involve initiative, time, commitment and sacrifice.

Never let your helpfulness detract from your own work or success. It's good that you want to help others. Just don't let anyone take up so much of your time that your own progress suffers. In business and career terms, it's best to put yourself first. The more successful you make yourself, the more help you can offer to others.

Don't Work For Nothing

If you're a performer or an entertainer, or if you provide any type of service, people will sometimes ask you to work for nothing. Often, they say something like: "We can't offer any money but it will be good exposure for you."

This isn't true. They're just trying to get you to work for nothing.

Sometimes, even television production people will feed you the same line, which is ridiculous. One appearance on one TV show won't make any difference to your career at all. Since everyone else involved in making the show gets paid, you should as well. It's a bit odd if the camera man, the production assistant and everyone else is getting some money but, curiously, there's none left for you.

In some rare circumstances, there might be a reason to perform on TV for no money. You might want to do it so that you can record the show when it's broadcast and use your appearance for promotional purposes. A video clip of you appearing on the show might make you look good in some people's eyes.

However, as a general rule, avoid working for nothing. When you go to the supermarket to buy food, they don't let you pay with good wishes or 'exposure'. They ask you for money. So that's what people need to give you when you perform or provide your service.

Bona fide charity work is a little different but even then you've got to be careful. If the organiser, the caterer and the cleaner are all getting paid, you should get paid as well. It doesn't mean you're uncaring or not supporting the needy. You are helping the event to be successful. You can donate your services for free if you want to but it's usually very counter-productive.

One final point: with rare exceptions, people don't appreciate what they get for free. It's a very sad fact but it's mostly true.

I've done countless charity gigs in my time (as have most self-employed people I know) but I always ask for a token fee. If they ask why, I say it's because people don't appreciate what they get for free. There's nothing to stop me donating my token fee to the charity the day after, if that's what I want to do. But I don't want to go along with the notion that my time and talent is literally worth nothing.

Some accountants would suggest there's another good reason to charge a token fee: it creates a paper trail of the transaction. The tax authorities like it if you keep everything visible and above board.

Don't Compete On Price

Competing on price is a *really* bad idea. Unfortunately, it's something that many people are tempted to do when they first start working for themselves.

When you're trying to get established, there may be times when you have to compromise a *little* on price. If you're running a business, you might trim your fees slightly or provide some extra value, just to get your first few customers. If you're an entertainer, you might agree to do some free or low-fee gigs to get experience, some photos of you in action, some quotes and some client names. Always be very careful about this because it can backfire horribly. Don't get stuck in the 'I'm a cheap act' zone. Have a fee and stick to it.

What should your fee be? At first, charge whatever is the market rate for what you do. To find out what the market rate is, ask your mentor and other people who do the sort of thing you do. Don't ask them how much *they* charge. That's not the point. Ask them how much *you* should charge, given that you're less experienced, you're just getting started and you're trying to build up your experience.

You may wonder why competing on price such a terrible idea. After all, isn't it just fair competition? Isn't it just one more way in which you can try to get some work and generate a little income? Well, actually, no.

When you compete on price, you are undervaluing yourself and teaching your clients to regard you as a cheap option. Once you have encouraged people to see you as 'cheap', they'll never see you any other way. It's not a good reputation to have. You are also encouraging clients to pay lower fees to everyone else in the same market, which won't exactly win you many friends.

In every market, there is room for a 'budget' level of service. There is room for flexibility, especially when you're trying to establish yourself and get your business off the ground. Nonetheless, try not to get caught in the trap of people only hiring you when you're cheap. There is no future in this.

Your goal is not to establish yourself as someone that's cheap. Your goal is to get to the point where people pay a lot of money for what you do because they appreciate the value that you provide. Competing on price is not the way forward and leads to meagre profits.

Compete on value. Compete on excellence. Compete on how useful you are to the person you're talking to. As the old saying goes, "Quality is remembered long after the price is forgotten."

Respect The Legalities

Whatever your line of work, it's part of your job to understand your legal responsibilities. For example, performers need to know about public liability insurance, musicians and artists need to understand copyright law and inventors need to learn how patents work.

Your mentor can help you with this (assuming you've managed to find one) but they may not be legally qualified to advise you. Whatever advice you need, book an appointment with someone suitably qualified to provide it. This doesn't have to be expensive. For example, there's a European company called Keltie that helps people to protect intellectual property rights. They offer a completely free first consultation.

Follow 'Standard' Practice

What sort of arrangement should you have with your clients, customers and people who hire you? Should you have everything covered by a contract to make sure you get paid? Or is it okay to do business on a handshake and a promise?

The answer is that every case is different. There are many different markets and cultures, hence many different versions of 'standard practice'. Some people always insist on a signed contract, others never use contracts at all.

See what your mentor suggests and learn from their experience. Never try to apply advice that comes from a different market, a different culture or a different part of the world.

Incidentally, even if you do insist on a written agreement every time you work with a client, this doesn't necessarily mean you need a professional legal contract. In most situations, any court of law will accept a clearly written agreement that was witnessed by a third party. (At least this is true in the UK, where I live.)

You just have to assess each case on its merits. The more money there is at stake, the more sensible it is to make sure you have a binding contract. If you do consult a legal expert, they can help you to draw up standard contracts you can use time and time again.

Sometimes you may not be able to get details in writing. There are entire businesses that operate on 'a word and a nod'. But do it whenever you can. It's good to know you have legally enforceable paperwork showing how much you'll get paid, when, who is legally responsible for paying you and how to contact them.

This is especially important if you do some work outside your own country. It's difficult to force people to pay what they owe when you're a long way away.

Here's another point to bear in mind if you're working for an overseas client: always stipulate in writing that when they pay you, by Paypal or direct bank transfer, they pay all the processing and currency conversion fees at *their* end. Otherwise, these fees can take a big bite out of your earnings.

If someone wants to do business with you but won't agree to put all the details in writing then you have to make a judgment call. Is the opportunity worth the risk to you? I'm not saying many people will try to avoid paying you. This isn't true. You can do lots of work without a contract and get paid satisfactorily. Nonetheless, attention to paperwork helps.

Don't Get Stuck In Legal Hell

Most people are fair, honest and easy to work with. However, once in a while you may do business with someone who owes you money but refuses to pay up.

Here's some advice.

First of all, even if the amount involved is relatively small, don't be too quick to just shrug and write it off to experience. If they get away with not paying you, they'll probably treat other people the same way. It's in everyone's interests to discourage dishonest and unfair trading.

Start by taking the normal steps to try to get them to pay up. Try asking, insisting and reasoning with them. Be persistent and make it clear that you're not just going to let them get away with it. However, never behave in an aggressive way. You can be assertive while also being calm, dignified and reasonable.

If this doesn't work, in rare cases you may decide the amount involved is so small that it's not worth taking legal action. Even if this is so, you can at least try to warn other people not to deal with this dishonest person. However, be very careful not to break the laws concerning slander, libel and defamation.

If you figure the amount you're owed is too large to forget about, or you just want to pursue the matter on principle, then you'll have to seek legal redress. If you have access to free legal advice (which some local councils and authorities do provide for small businesses), take it. Don't assume it's necessarily expensive to pursue legal action. Do some research and look into the legal options open to you. I live in England, where you can go online and issue a claim against someone who owes you money (www.moneyclaim.gov.uk). It doesn't cost much. You just have to say why the other party owes you money and provide your evidence. There may be similar options available in your part of the world.

You may also think of joining a business or professional group that provides legal advice to its members. For example, here in the UK we have something called the Federation of Small Businesses, which any entrepreneur can join. Among other benefits, members can get free legal guidance whenever they want it. There may be similar groups or associations that you would find useful.

Many people pay up as soon as you take the first legal step to claim what you're owed. They don't want to deal with legal proceedings or get bad judgments made against them.

However, if you're thinking of taking more substantial legal action, be careful. Significant legal cases can take an absurdly long time to go through the courts. It could be years before you get a result. Even if you have a watertight case, there's no certainty that you'll win because legal matters can be very unpredictable.

Should you happen to win your case, and the court tells the other party to pay you, it could be a long time before you actually see the money. If they simply refuse to pay up, you'll need to go back through the legal system to get the payment enforced. What's more, even if you get the money awarded to you, this might be less than your legal expenses. All in all, think very carefully before taking substantial legal action. It could hold you back for a very long time with no guarantee that the stress will be worth it.

When it comes to legal matters, the only people who really win are the lawyers. Don't get stuck in legal hell.

Be Careful About TV

If you are a performer or an entertainer, and if you want to become well known, getting on TV can help (although it isn't essential).

However, let me give you some advice. The practicalities of TV production mean that your time and participation can often end up being wasted. This isn't because TV production people are unkind. They are usually great people who do difficult work under a lot of pressure. Nonetheless, it's all too easy to end up feeling rather dismayed.

Example 1

They contact you about doing an interview. It takes a while to set the whole thing up. On the eve of the interview they call to say they've had to change the plan. On the rescheduled day, you do the interview. It lasts for about fifteen minutes but it has taken up an entire afternoon of your time. When the interview is broadcast, it has been heavily edited and you're on screen for about ten seconds. Or you're edited out completely.

Example 2

They invite you to take part in a topical discussion show. They say you need to be at the studio at 11 am for technical rehearsals and production discussions. You turn up and wait all day. None of the rehearsals or discussions they mentioned ever take place. Eventually, at 7 pm, they start taping the show. You're involved for about a minute. When the show is broadcast, even this has been edited down to a few seconds.

Example 3

They invite you to take part in a show all about your area of expertise. They assure you that your contribution will be very welcome. You turn up at the appointed time and hang around for ages. It's getting close to show time. A production assistant takes you to one side and explains, very apologetically, that they won't be able to use you because they have more guests or panellists than they actually need. They say you can stay and watch the show but you won't actually be featured at all.

All of these examples are from real life. More specifically, they are all from *my* life! All these things have happened to me and to many of my self-employed friends in the world of entertainment. However, I hasten to add that I've also had many *good* experiences of working with television people.

These things don't happen because of incompetence or malice. Making a TV show isn't easy and sometimes people end up disappointed. For example, TV people routinely overbook guests for discussion shows because they're worried that some might cancel at short notice and they'll be left without enough people. If they need, say, six people for the show, they book ten just to cover themselves. From their point of view, having more people than they really need isn't a problem. If you're one of the ones that get dropped the whole thing will have been a waste of *your* time but not theirs. This is just an unfortunate consequence of how TV shows are made.

All that having been said, participating in TV shows can be fun and very useful. I have taken part in lots of TV shows, dating back to the 1990s. I have hours of clips, appearances, interviews and performances. Some of the shows were great to be involved with and I have very happy memories of both the shows themselves and the people I met.

Consultancy roles can also work out well. I've been a consultant on about half a dozen TV shows (mostly related to the magic world) and in most cases it's been a very enjoyable experience. I was a consultant on a magic and mindreading show in Finland, for the wonderful Noora Strömsholm, that was so much fun I would have happily ignored my own advice and worked on it for nothing!

All I'm saying is that you should be careful. TV isn't quite the magical wonderland of opportunities that many people think it is. Being involved with a TV show can absorb a lot of your time and spirit and leave you with not much to show for it.

Take care.

* * *

What's Next?

You're going to face criticism from time to time so learning to handle it well is essential. This is the subject if the next chapter, which includes the valuable lesson of The Two Dresses!

15. Dealing With Criticism

"Adopt the pace of nature: her secret is patience."

— Ralph Waldo Emerson

15. Dealing With Criticism

When you work for yourself, you will inevitably face criticism. This is especially true if you are a performer or if you do anything artistic or creative. It's just part of the deal. You can't escape it any more than you can escape air.

Knowing how to handle criticism successfully can be a crucial factor in your success. Here's the best advice I can offer.

The 10:10:80 Principle

Whoever you are, and whatever you do, in the course of your career you will encounter more or less the same range of reactions. Assuming you have at least a modicum of talent or ability, you'll find that it breaks down like this:

- Roughly 10% of people will think you're great.

- Roughly 10% will think you're terrible.

- The other 80% don't have a strong opinion either way.
  They've got their own heap of cares and concerns and
  you're just not a very big dot on their radar.

These percentages don't tend to vary a great deal. When you hear about a pop star having millions of loyal and adoring fans, remember that there are probably just as many millions of people who can't stand him or her. Conversely, if you know of a local pub band with about ten fans, they probably don't have many people who hate them either. The two sides of this equation tend to grow equally. Putting it another way, popularity tends to maintain equilibrium.

This was all put into perspective for me by a wonderful interview I read, over thirty years ago, with pop star Gary Numan. At the time, Gary had sold about a million copies of his debut album and a journalist asked him how he felt about it. Gary said that it was obviously very nice but it was worth keeping a sense of perspective. As he explained, given that the population of the UK was about 60 million, if one million people had bought his album then 59 million people had either never heard of him or they *had* heard his stuff and had actively chosen *not* to buy it! I thought this was a very refreshing way of looking at it.

In this section, I'd like to suggest a few other ways to handle any criticism that comes your way.

Two Quotations

I have always loved this quotation, which seems to me to be a good, solid answer to 99% of all criticism. It comes from a good source:

> "If I were to try to read, much less answer, all the attacks made on me, this shop might as well be closed for any other business. I do the very best I know how — the very best I can — and I mean to keep on doing so until the end. If the end brings me out all right, what is said against me won't amount to anything. If the end brings me out wrong, ten angels swearing I was right would make no difference."
> — Abraham Lincoln

And here's one more:

> "Taking to pieces is the trade of those who cannot construct."
> — R. W. Emerson

(As it happens, Emerson wasn't actually referring to negative criticism. This quotation is from 'Natural Method of Mental Philosophy, Lecture III: Powers of the Mind', in which Emerson says the analytical mind, which likes to 'take apart', has given us less than the artistic mind, which prefers to create. Nonetheless, I mention this quote whenever people are troubled by negative comments. It seems to fit.)

Learn If You Can, Ignore If You Can't

Not all criticism is created equal.

If criticism is both informed and constructive, then it's actually very useful stuff. You can learn a lot from it. Always welcome this kind of criticism and see it as a great opportunity for improvement. There have been many times in my own life when some intelligent criticism has proved to be of significant benefit.

If criticism fails either of these tests — if it isn't well informed, or isn't constructive — then it is literally useless, like a rubber tuning fork. You couldn't do anything useful with it even if you wanted to. It may be offered with good intentions but it's useless all the same.

You don't need to get angry about useless criticism or start arguing about it. There's no need for a fight, a sulk or a tantrum, none of which would achieve anything anyway. Your only real option is to shrug, accept that you can't do anything with this particular bit of criticism and then quietly ignore it.

The Two Dresses Syndrome

A man buys his wife two dresses for her birthday. When they get ready to go out that evening, she puts one of them on. He immediately snaps at her, "What's wrong with the other one?!"

When you work for yourself, there will be times when you can only choose either option A or option B. As soon as you make your choice, critics and self-appointed 'experts' will point out that you could have chosen the alternative. This has often happened to me in my career as a freelance writer. On more than a few projects, I've been faced with two options:

(A) Simple and easy to read but lacking in detail.

(B) Lots of detail but longer to read and harder to absorb.

If I took the first option, people would say, "It's all right I suppose, but you know you've missed out a lot of detail that I feel needs to be there. If you're just going to gloss over the details, there's not much point."

If I took the second option, they'd say, "It's okay, but I think most people would find it difficult to get through. Can't you make it easier to read? You're supposed to be good at explaining things in simple terms. People haven't got all day, you know."

You can't please everyone. If you have to choose between two options, there will always be someone who suggests the alternative would have been better. They often do this in a rather condescending tone, as if they (in two minutes) have thought the matter through more carefully than you (after you've been working on the project for three weeks).

Some people *have* to comment on your work because it's part of their job. If they didn't find anything to say they would be admitting that they serve no real purpose. Since they have to say *something*, suggesting the opposite of whatever you've done is the easiest option.

There's no easy solution to this. If you're being paid to do some work, the person paying you is in charge. You either have to do as they wish or go through the very delicate, diplomatic exercise of explaining why it's best if you don't.

I'm mentioning the Two Dresses Syndrome so that if you encounter it you will know it doesn't just happen to you. It's not really 'criticism', as such. It's just people finding something to say because they have to or because they want to feel a bit superior.

Opinion And Judgment

There are two kinds of criticism: opinion and judgment.

The first kind of criticism is opinion. It sounds like this: "I don't like that very much."

Of course, everyone is entitled to their opinion. You are free to say whether or not you like something and so am I. However, opinion has very little to do with *merit*. By any relevant criteria, Jane Austen wrote some of the greatest novels ever written which is why she's so enduringly popular. Even so, I'd rather jab a fork in my eye than read any of her work — it's just not what I enjoy. In similar vein, one of my friends is highly educated and a classically trained musician. He openly admits that he can't stand the music of Mozart. The scythe of harsh opinion cuts us all the same.

The second kind of criticism is judgment. It sounds like this: "That isn't very good."

This is quite distinct from saying "I don't like it" (which is a perfectly legitimate opinion). Anyone declaring, "That person isn't doing that thing very well" is offering their *judgment*.

If this judgment comes from someone who knows what they are talking about, their view should be respected. In particular, if it's from someone who understands the challenges involved in whatever you're discussing, whether it's playing jazz saxophone or setting up a new retail operation, they are in a position to offer an *informed* judgment based on past experience. Given that they understand the challenges involved, their judgment is probably worth listening to.

If this is not the case, and the words come from someone who lacks any relevant insight or personal experience, there is no reason to respect their judgment at all. Since they don't understand the challenges involved in whatever is being discussed, they cannot possibly offer much by way of sound judgment. They may have an *opinion* about whether or not they *like* whatever is being discussed. However, they are not in any position to form a judgment. (At least, not a judgment that deserves any attention.)

When you work for yourself, I think it's always a good idea to bear this distinction in mind. Everyone is entitled to their *opinion*. Not everyone is able to offer good *judgment*.

The BITDIG Principle

Suppose you try to do something difficult, such as trying your hand at a bit of stand-up comedy. You write your set, learn it, go along to the gig and do your five minutes. Furthermore, suppose quite a lot of people tell you afterwards that you weren't very good.

How should you feel about this?

I think you should feel magnificently proud of yourself for actually having *tried*. The people offering their opinion haven't done anything difficult. Anyone can sit in a chair and say, "You're no good." This takes literally no skill, effort or talent.

To actually get up on the stage and try to perform is *far* more difficult and a tremendous challenge. Even if you try and fail, and hardly anyone laughed, you have far more to be proud of than the person who didn't even try.

One of my favourite films is 'One Flew Over The Cuckoo's Nest', which came out in 1975. It contains the scene in which Randle McMurphy (played by Jack Nicholson) bets the other characters that he can lift something extremely heavy. Despite all his bravura confidence, he fails. The others feel smug and superior, jeering at McMurphy and openly mocking his failure.

McMurphy walks past them all, by now thoroughly exhausted and apparently beaten. Just before he leaves, he turns to face his tormentors and offers one parting comment: "But I *tried*, didn't I, goddammit? At least I did *that!*"

Suddenly, the scene is transformed. The loser now seems like the winner and vice-versa. None of the others even had the spirit to try. At least McMurphy got that far. Although he failed, he has more to be proud of than those who didn't even try.

This scene changed my life. It's one of the factors that encouraged me to go on my journey into the world of self-employment. Sometimes, I've enjoyed a bit of success. At other times, I've failed. However, I've always remembered this wonderful line.

This is what I call the BITDIG principle. It stands for, "But I tried, didn't I, goddammit!"

Incidentally, if you have seen 'Cuckoo's Nest' but haven't read the novel by Ken Kesey on which it's based, I highly recommend you check it out. It is, by any standards, a remarkable piece of writing.

146

Goldman's Beautiful Advice

William Goldman was a very successful novelist and screenwriter. He wrote a truly majestic book called 'Adventures In The Screen Trade', all about his experience of working in Hollywood and writing screenplays. Quite early in the book, Goldman says there's one thing everyone needs to know about the movie business: nobody knows anything.

Goldman's point is that many Hollywood people think they know how to make a successful movie. In fact, some executives get paid to act as if they know how. However, it's all bogus, as the book makes clear.

This is why every single year, the TV and movie studios churn out stuff that they are sure is going to work, based on their expert judgment, and it flops horribly (losing a heap of money in the process). On the flip side, there are always small, tiny projects, rejected by everyone, that somehow get produced and become hugely popular.

When you work for yourself, especially if you do anything creative, you will meet people who think they know what will or will not work. In all probability, they don't. To paraphrase Goldman: nobody knows anything but the market knows everything.

All you can do is create what you want to create, get the word out, put in the effort and see what the market tells you. Sometimes the market says yes, we like your stuff and we want what you're offering. Good! Sometimes the market says no, we're not interested. Good! You've learned something. This means you can try again with another idea, this time with the added benefit of experience.

You can try to get an idea of what the market wants via market research. This is a specialised field in its own right and beyond the scope of this book. However, you should be aware that market research is far from straightforward. Here are just three common difficulties.

First of all, people can't want what they don't know about. Nobody knew they wanted a smart phone before smart phones were invented.

Secondly, 'want' doesn't always translate to 'buy'. People might say they'd like your product to have some fancy extra features. However, if adding those features means greater manufacturing costs, so the price goes up, people might reject the new price.

Thirdly, people often give what they think are the 'right' answers rather than honest or accurate ones. Lots of people say they respect ethical or environmental concerns when in reality these factors never affect their buying decisions.

Turning Down The Beatles

One aspect of 'nobody knows anything' is that so-called 'experts' make terrible decisions all the time. The history of the entertainment industry is littered with examples of decision-makers who made terrible mistakes. Perhaps most famously of all, Decca records turned down The Beatles in 1962. They said, "We don't like their sound, and guitar music is on the way out."

There are many similar stories from the world of business and industry. If you search online for 'famous business blunders', you can spend many happy hours reading about large, successful companies making decisions so bad they required a special kind of genius. Ford thinking the world would love the Edsel, Coca-Cola launching 'New Coke', Kodak ignoring the potential of digital photography... the list goes on and on. Enjoy reading these stories and remember: nobody knows anything, the market knows everything.

My Favourite Example

The music of Mike Oldfield has played an important role in my life. Oldfield's incredible work ignited my love for music and is also the reason I taught myself to play the guitar. Oldfield's story is one of my favourite examples of admirable creative persistence in the face of more or less universal rejection.

By his late teens, Oldfield was earning a modest living as a rock guitarist and bass player. However, he had an idea for a highly unusual album that he'd like to make. It was going to be entirely instrumental, no words or songs. Instead of individual 'tracks', the album would be a collage of musical ideas, drawing on many different styles and influences, each section blending subtly into the next. Even the way Mike wanted to make the album was unusual: he intended to play most of the different parts himself, using the magic of multi-track recording to layer them all together and create the sounds he wanted.

Mike made a short demo tape of his ideas and took it to everyone he could find in the music industry. Nobody was interested. For two years, he knocked on doors, played his tape and explained his idea. Everyone told him it wouldn't sell and that he was wasting his time.

Eventually, Richard Branson gave Oldfield enough studio time to actually make the record. Branson then tried to find a record label willing to sell this unusual album of instrumental music. Nobody wanted it. Everyone said it had no commercial potential. Branson finally put the album out himself as the first release on the Virgin record label.

148

'Tubular Bells', as the album was called, went on to be one of the biggest albums of the 70s, selling millions and millions of copies internationally and staying on the UK music charts for 279 weeks. It launched Oldfield's career and, some would say, also established an entirely new genre of contemporary instrumental music. Not bad for a record that the experts said had no commercial potential whatsoever!

If you don't know Mike Oldfield's music, you may like to check out some of his work. In particular, I recommend an album called 'Ommadawn'. This is the piece of music I know better than any other and it was a major source of inspiration to my younger self. If there had been no 'Ommadawn', this book wouldn't exist.

* * *

What's Next?

It's time to discuss the rather fascinating subject of making money. This next section involves an old joke and something interesting that happens in a coffee shop.

16. About Making Money

"Whoever said money can't buy happiness didn't know where to shop."

— Gertrude Stein

16. About Making Money

Nobody decides to be self-employed purely to make money. Personal fulfilment can't be measured by numbers on a bank account. However, making money is generally part of the plan.

This being the case, you may have noticed this book's glaring deficiency. It does not come with a magic wand that, when you wave it around in a suitably theatrical fashion, guarantees that money will fall out of the sky into your pockets. Also missing from this edition: a golden duck that grants wishes and a fully functional money magnet.

The reason I don't supply any of these things is because, as you know, they don't exist. You may think this is obvious and I agree that it *should* be. Sadly, even today many people can be persuaded to believe otherwise — hence the endless parade of 'get rich quick' books, schemes and websites (which I'll address later in this book).

In this chapter, I won't offer you any 'get rich quick' absurdity, nor will I suggest that if you just ask the universe nicely enough it will shower you with riches. Instead, I just want to give you the best and most realistic advice I can about making money. For me, it all comes down to an important difference between a 'get' and 'allow' mentality.

Mental Blocks (1)

Before I can talk about making money, I have to mention some of the mental blocks that often get in the way.

The first type of mental block has to do with self-limiting beliefs. For one reason or another, some people have an inner conviction that they don't *deserve* financial success or are not entitled to it. Even people who say they'd like to be wealthy often behave in a way that betrays self-limiting and self-denying beliefs. There's a conflict between their words and their behaviour. They may say they'd like more money but never take any steps towards this goal and instead move in the opposite direction, sabotaging their own opportunities.

If you don't believe you're entitled to be wealthy, you never will be. You will never take steps to make money because you've already decided you don't deserve to have any. It's therefore essential to get past whatever self-limiting beliefs might block your progress. If necessary, see a qualified therapist. Understand that you are entitled to wealth and the good things it can provide. Otherwise, the rest of this chapter is going to be rather pointless.

Mental Blocks (2)

The second type of mental block consists of 'straw man' arguments that people never seem to tire of flinging at any discussion to do with making money. Let's deal with a few of them.

'Money can't buy happiness'

This is one of the most unhelpfully inane utterances I've ever come across. It's true that happiness is not a commodity. You can't go to the store and ask for a bottle of it. However, you can use money to buy things that will greatly increase your level of happiness. To say money can't buy happiness is like saying you can't eat money — true, but you can use money to buy some really nice things to eat.

It's time to kill off this 'money can't buy happiness' nonsense once and for all.

There are two types of problems in life: ones that money can solve and ones that money can't. If you don't have money, you have to deal with both types of problems. If you have money, you only have to deal with one type.

There are two types of nice, pleasant and enjoyable things in life: ones that money can buy and ones that money can't. If you don't have money, you only have one type in your life. If you have money, you can have both.

Either way you slice it, *having* money is a better deal, and gives you more choice and freedom, than *not* having it.

'It's wrong to have an unhealthy obsession with money'

Agreed, and I'm not suggesting otherwise. Any 'unhealthy obsession' is, by definition, best avoided. I wouldn't want to have an unhealthy obsession with cactus plants or rainbows either. So what?

'Having money doesn't mean your life will be perfect.'

Wealth isn't a door to an idyllic life of peaches and sunshine. Having money won't make you nicer, more intelligent or likeable. There will still be rainy days, stubbed toes and trains that run late. Nonetheless, I'd rather be unhappy while sitting on a comfy sofa in a nice, warm house than while being homeless and starving.

Let's keep it simple. In general terms, money is pretty useful and more is generally preferable to less. After all, if you've got too much you can give some away. If you have too little, you have fewer options.

Incidentally, you can't only use money to buy *things*. You can also use it to buy *experiences*, which is more likely to lead to long-term happiness. When I look back over recent years, not many *things* I've bought have made me significantly happier. However, I am delighted that I've seen the Penguin Parade at Phillip Island, had several trips to Las Vegas, explored the Hofburg Palace in Vienna, done some eye-opening shifts at 'Crisis' (the homeless charity), visited the statue of Christ The Redeemer in Rio, enjoyed the botanical gardens of Kuala Lumpur and seen Tchaikovsky's 'Onegin' at the Mariinsky's Theatre in Moscow. Money enabled me to have these fantastic experiences and more.

Even if you're not interested in having money to buy things, think about the 'wealth' of great experiences it can place within your reach.

Two Lessons

Let's assume you aren't plagued by mental blocks and you can see past the 'money can't buy happiness' nonsense. Good! What's next?

I want to share two lessons. Lesson #1 involves an old joke and Lesson #2 is about coffee shops. I promise there's a point to these two stories.

Lesson #1: The Church Joke

A man goes to church and prays. "Lord, I have been a faithful servant to you all my life. I have worked hard but I am poor. Please, let me win the lottery. It is all I ask." A week goes by. He goes back to the church and beseeches God even more passionately than before. "Lord, I have been a good and faithful servant to you all my life. I have worked hard but I am still poor. Please, please let me win the lottery. It is all I ask."

Another week goes by. He goes to the church a third time and prays in an even more impassioned way. "Lord, I have been a good and faithful servant to you all my life. I have worked hard, but I am very, very poor. Please, please, please let me win the lottery. It is all I ask." At that moment, a great light fills the church and the air is filled with the sound of heavenly choirs. God's voice booms down at the man: "Hey, meet me halfway... would you at least *buy a ticket?*"

It's an old joke with a simple lesson: if you want something to happen, you have to take the steps that will *allow* it to happen.

Lesson #2: The Coffee Shop Scene

One of my simple pleasures in life is hanging out in coffee shops. I don't actually drink coffee, only tea, but I love meeting up and chatting with friends and clients while the world goes by outside.

It's worth sitting in a coffee shop for a while and observing what happens: complete strangers literally walk in off the street and give their money to the coffee shop. The shop doesn't have staff out on the street pleading with people to come in and spend money. They don't beg the general public, "Oh, please come in and give us some money." They don't have to do this. They just open the shop each morning and it happens.

Of course, the coffee shop has had to do a lot of work to reach this point. They've had to find suitable premises, get the place fitted out, devise the menu, sort out the supply and delivery chain, hire staff, see to all the marketing, keep up with all the admin and attend to a hundred other aspects of their business operation. It's a huge amount of work. However, once they've done all these things, people just walk in and give them money. The people running the coffee shop have taken the steps that *allow* this to happen.

Allow It To Happen

The Church Joke and the Coffee Shop scene convey a simple point: if you want something nice to happen in your life, you have to take the steps that *allow* it to happen. If you think this is obvious, all I can say is that it can't be *that* obvious because millions of people don't seem to realise it.

When I give talks, I sometimes ask the audience, "Would you like to earn a thousand pounds in a single day?" Everyone says yes. Then I ask, "Okay, would you like to earn a thousand pounds in a single day without even doing any work?" Everyone says yes again. Next, I ask, "Well, what steps have you taken to allow this to happen in your life?" At this point, the room tends to be rather quiet.

I know what it's like to earn a thousand pounds in a day without doing any work. Why? Because I took the steps that allow it to happen. First of all, I had to learn about 'passive income' and how e-commerce websites work. Then I had to set up my site and create products to put on it. Having got that far, I had to learn how to market the website and promote it. This all took a long time. In fact, because I'm not very bright and made a lot of mistakes, it took me several years. However, I do now have e-commerce websites that *sometimes* generate over a thousand pounds in a single day.

Please understand that I am not trying to impress you. I am not saying I've done anything smart, admirable or heroic. Quite the opposite. I'm saying I took simple steps that anyone could take. I wanted something to happen so I took the steps that *allow* it to happen. That's the only point I'm making.

(It perhaps also helped that five years ago I switched off my TV and ditched it at the local recycling centre. However, I'm not suggesting this is an essential step.)

Jack And Jill

Jack is an entertainer. He sits at home, practising his skills in front of a mirror. He keeps fervently hoping that one day, by some weird miracle, someone will discover his awesome talent.

Jill is also an entertainer. She has put together a good act and created some attractive publicity material. She has presentable photos and videos of herself in action. She has a website that is fairly simple but tells people who she is, what she does and why they might want to hire her. She has contacted every agent, booker and producer she could think of to get work and she makes dozens of marketing calls every week. She has slowly developed her network of fellow performers (who might occasionally have a lead or an opportunity for her). She works hard and takes every opportunity she can to develop her talent.

One day, out of the blue, someone calls and offers Jill a truly excellent gig that's fun to do and pulls in a big fee. Jack thinks, "She's so *lucky*. Why can't that happen to me?"

The difference is that Jill has taken the steps that allow it to happen. There is no guarantee that if you take the right steps, the good things you want will happen. Life is a casino and by definition you can't control luck. However, you can be absolutely certain that if you do *not* take the right steps the nice things will *not* happen.

There are rare exceptions because there are exceptions to everything. Some people make little effort but enjoy big rewards. People like this are weird, statistical flukes. Don't base your life and expectations on weird flukes. Go with what the overwhelming majority of examples indicate: good things happen in your life when you put in the work that *allows* them to happen.

By the way, Jack and Jill are real people that I happen to know quite well. Obviously, I've changed their names but they are not just imaginary examples.

'Get' Versus 'Allow'

I think a lot of people, when they start working for themselves, feel as if they are *grasping* for money and trying to *persuade* people to hand it over. "Please hire me, book me, buy my product. Please give me some of your money."

The 'allow' mentality feels very different. People who have money *want* to spend it on things because money by itself is rather dull. It's only useful when it is actually spent on something. The people who walk into the coffee shop don't need to be begged to spend money. They perceive some value in having a nice cup of coffee and a place to enjoy it, so they happily walk up to the counter and hand over their cash.

If you offer people something they want, and you get the word out, you'll have the same experience. You won't need to do much to get money from people — they will quite happily hand it over. Your job is to take the steps that *allow* this to happen.

So, if you want to work for yourself, and you wonder how you'll make money, this is my answer. You work out the value that people want (in a particular market) and do your best to provide it, thereby *allowing* their money to come to you.

Not Just Playing With Words

This difference between the 'get' and 'allow' mentality is not just a case of playing with words. I sincerely believe it's an important distinction that has helped me and many of the people that I mentor.

Suppose your attitude sounds like this: "What can I do to persuade people to give me some of their money?"

When you express yourself in this way, you are casting yourself in a low-status role. You sound needy, passive and receptive, hoping for someone to give you some money almost as if you're holding out a begging bowl. None of this feels very nice on a psychological or emotional level.

In contrast, suppose this is your attitude: "People *want* to give me money because of the value I provide. I just have to take the right steps to allow this to happen."

This time, you are casting yourself in a high-status role: someone that people actually want to give money to! You are not needy, passive or receptive and you're not pleading with anyone. You are taking an active role, using your initiative and other resources to take the steps that allow what you want to happen. You are not persuading anyone so much as providing what people want and will willingly pay for. This all feels much nicer and more positive in emotional terms.

This is why I believe the 'allow' mentality makes a difference. It changes how you feel about yourself, your role and your potential. It gives you a much more positive outlook, eliminating a lot of negativity that could sabotage your own success.

The difference between 'get' and 'allow' is not a magic spell that will just make money appear out of thin air. I can't offer you that and neither can anyone else. However, I do think the 'allow' mentality can transform your outlook so you're more likely to take the right steps to allow money to come to you. Why not try it and see?

Making And Sticking

My first boss was a very experienced businessman. In his time he had done just about everything: run his own construction firm, owned a chain of shops, sold cars, played in a band, owned a petrol station and set up a video studio. He often used to say, "Making money isn't the problem. Anyone can make a bit of money. The problem is making some of it *stick*." These are wise words.

People who are thinking of working for themselves sometimes worry about whether they'll get *any* customers or generate any income at all. With very rare exceptions, this isn't something you need to be concerned about. The fact is, if you're offering any half-decent product or service, you will almost certainly have some money coming in. A business venture would have to be quite spectacularly misguided not to get *any* customers at all.

However, you'll find that money has an annoying tendency to go out just as quickly as it comes in. Just when you think you're doing well and your monthly revenue looks pretty good, you add up all your costs and expenses and realise you haven't made a single penny of profit. In other words, you've nothing to show for all your hard work.

You have to be careful about this. Always keep track of the money coming in *and* the money going out. Don't kid yourself that your outgoings are lower than they really are just to feel better about the situation. At the end of each week or month, ask yourself if you've managed to save any of the money that came in. If not, then you only have two options. You either need to increase how much is coming in or decrease how much is going out. This is commercial reality.

A Few More Money Notes

In this chapter, we've looked at some mental blocks that get in the way of making money and explored the subtle yet crucial difference between 'get' and 'allow'.

I'm sorry if this doesn't strike you as very exciting advice. It won't appeal to anyone who believes there's a mystical, magical 'get rich quick' path to wealth that they'll find if they just buy enough books, listen to enough podcasts and go to enough seminars. (Spoiler alert: there is no such path and you'll go broke trying to find it.)

Nonetheless, while it may seem unexciting, it is the best advice I can offer you after working for myself for over twenty years and enjoying every second of every day. I'm not a millionaire (yet) but I seem to enjoy quite a nice life and somehow survive despite living in an absurdly expensive city.

Just before I close this chapter, I'd like to mention a few additional points about making money that you may find interesting. Take whatever you find useful and ignore the rest.

Putting Your Prices Up

If you do any kind of freelance work, especially if you're an entertainer or performer, you will sooner or later face an interesting question: how do you know when to put your prices up? After all, nobody likes to feel they're charging less than they *could* be charging.

The answer is that the market will tell you. When you start off, charge whatever seems to be the going rate for what you do. When you've got a full diary, and more bookings are coming in than you can handle, that's when you know you can put your prices up a bit. Put them up by about 10% and see what happens.

Repeat this process as appropriate. As soon as you have a full diary and you're getting more enquiries than you can handle, raise your rates by another 10%. You don't need to worry about if and when to put your prices up. The demand for your services tells you everything you need to know. Remember: nobody knows anything but the market knows everything.

You can apply the same reasoning to almost any other kind of business, whether you run a home decorating service, sell ceramic cats or make novelty wedding cakes. The market, and the state of your order book, will tell you if the time has come to put your prices up.

A Note About Advertising

Since this chapter is about making money, I have to mention the subject of advertising. There are people who suggest it's absolutely *essential* to advertise if you want to make any money. By a staggering coincidence, these are very often people who work in advertising!

So, let's take a closer look.

Paid Advertising

A single advert is essentially pointless. It has been said that the average consumer has to see an advert seven times before they even notice it, let alone act on it.

Advertising is only effective when it is part of a coherent marketing strategy and when you can afford to sustain a campaign over several weeks or months. Needless to say, advertising campaigns can get very expensive, very quickly.

Where you advertise will obviously depend on who you want to reach. If your customers only read printed magazines and never go online, that's where you have to advertise. However, all other things being equal, and in lieu of any compelling reason to do otherwise, explore digital marketing and online advertising before you try anything else.

Google and social media sites such as Facebook provide extremely cost-effective and powerful advertising tools. In fact, their scale and power is actually rather scary when you get into the details. They allow you to target potential customers with extreme precision that traditional media cannot possibly hope to match. However, don't try to guess how to use these powerful resources wisely. You'll waste a lot of time and money. Either study them in detail or work with a digital marketing specialist who can show you how to use these tools effectively. You'll be amazed at what's possible!

Once you have looked into online promotion and advertising, you may want to also explore traditional print and media advertising. It all depends on what you do, where you'll find your customers and what you can afford. However, there can be no doubt: digital marketing is usually the more powerful option. This is just the age we live in.

It's also a good idea to ask other people in your field about effective advertising resources. For example, if there's a specialised, industry-specific website or trade directory that many people in your line of work say gets results, that's another option to explore.

___

Word-Of-Mouth Advertising (WOM)

Every advertising executive and marketing guru in the world will tell you the same thing: the best form of advertising is WOM: word-of-mouth. When *you* tell everyone you're great, you might perhaps win some customers. When *your customers* tell everyone you're great, you'll win many more.

You can't buy WOM but you can do two things to encourage it.

First, deliver a very high level of customer satisfaction. Treat your customers like people, not statistics on a sales spreadsheet. Charm them and always 'go the extra mile' to please them. Satisfied customers aren't enough. You want them to be *more* than satisfied. Make it your mission to under-promise and over-deliver. Behind everyone who buys anything from you, there are ten others who might. Give every customer good reasons to recommend you to the people they know.

Secondly, exploit every opportunity to tell people about your product, service, act or whatever it is you want people to pay for. Every conversation you have, whether in person, on the phone or online, is a chance to mention your product. How many conversations do you have in a month? In a year? Many of them are a chance to plant a seed that could lead to a sale. If you had planted as many seeds as possible last year, think of all the customers you'd have now. Take every chance you can, every day, to sow the seeds of more WOM.

Never underestimate the power of word-of-mouth advertising. It can work wonders and costs next to nothing.

A Note About Agents

I can't end this chapter about making money without mentioning the role of agents. You may be in a line of work where you have to have an agent, or 'representation', in order to get anywhere. If so, welcome to the minefield.

Good agents can get you to heaven. This is why they are in demand and can afford to be choosy. Bad agents can't get you a gig in a ditch. This is why they aren't in such demand and tend to be less selective.

If you want an agent, you may or may not be able to find one willing to represent you. If you find one willing to represent you, they may or may not be good at getting you lots of work. If you find one who gets you lots of work, they may deal with you fairly, or you may feel rather cheated and short-changed.

When the story works out happily, and you get a good agent who finds plenty of work for you and plays nice, it's great. Your agent can be an important ally in your success story and the two of you can be a good team. In all other cases (you can't get an agent, they're no good at finding work or they don't play fair), it's not so great.

It's important to understand that an agent is only interested in you to the extent that they can make money out of you. There's nothing cold and cynical about this. It's just what being an agent is all about.

Also, remember that agents are in business to earn money *for themselves*. The fact that you also benefit is incidental. So if the agent can send you to a gig for X, but can send someone else for a bigger fee (hence earning a bigger commission), they're going to send the other person. It's nothing personal. It's just business.

If you're unhappy with your agent, don't let the situation fester for a long time. Have a meeting, explain your grievances in a fair and reasonable way and see what happens. If the situation improves, fine. If not, it's time to move on and either find another agent or go it alone.

* * *

What's Next?

The next section is about success, or at least some of the mythology surrounding the subject. Among other things, it tells you everything you need to know about 'success secrets'!

17. Success Mythology

"What we call failure is not the falling down but the staying down."

— Mary Pickford

17. Success Mythology

If you work for yourself, and particularly if you are a performer of some description, you are probably quite interested in the notion of 'success' and how to achieve it. Unfortunately, it's a word entangled in a lot of unhelpful mythology. In this chapter, I want to address some of these myth-conceptions and the mechanisms behind them. Then you can go on to the next chapter, which is all about 'Success Reality'.

Myth #1: Get Rich Quick

The Get Rich Quick industry has always been with us and isn't going away anytime soon. It survives by feeding on an uncomfortable truth about the difference between what people *say* and what they *mean*. Some people *say* they want success. What they *mean* is they want some of the things they *associate* with success, such as wealth, *without* having to work for it or do anything very difficult or time-consuming.

Unfortunately, these people are doomed to disappointment. You can *believe* there's a way to achieve wealth without effort, just as you can believe in golden unicorns. You're free to believe whatever you want. However, you'll never find that unicorn. Positive thinking is great but it only works when it's in harmony with reality and practical experience.

Here's a classic example of Get Rich Quick mythology in action. Once upon a time, GRQ merchants ran ads in newspapers offering to share the secrets of easy wealth in return for a small fee. The intrigued reader clipped the coupon and sent off their money. All they got back was a letter suggesting that if they want to make easy money, they should put an ad in the paper promising to reveal their 'Get Rich Quick' secrets. "After all," the letter continued, "you have just proved that it works, haven't you?"

There are two points to note about this simple example of a Get Rich Quick operation. First of all, the GRQ maestro has nothing to offer except one idea: 'To make money, tell people you can teach them how to make money'. Secondly, it's easy to identify GRQ schemes because they all share the same glaring omission: no-one is providing any *value* to anyone else.

Every legitimate business is based on a seller providing *value* to a buyer. Of course, the value can take many different forms. Maybe you run a bakery or entertain people with your amazing contortionist act. Maybe you offer your neighbourhood's best laundry service or delight jazz fans around the world with your dazzling clarinet technique.

The details vary but the bedrock reality of fair exchange is always the same: you provide value that people are willing to pay for. GRQ mythology departs from this reality and suggests you can have one side (people give you money) without the other (you provide some value). This just ain't so. There are some rules and realities in life and you can't make rain fall upwards.

I expect that anyone reading this book is aware of all this and unlikely to be seduced by dazzling Get Rich Quick schemes. However, you need to stay vigilant because, as I said, GRQ mythology constantly re-invents itself to seduce each new generation of unicorn hunters.

For a while, its favourite camouflage was pyramid and Ponzi schemes. Then it was all about asking the universe to give you wealth. The internet era has given rise to a shiny new form of GRQ mythology. It's based on the idea that if you just learn enough about clever online marketing techniques, you can spin straw into gold and enjoy limitless wealth. This new, digital version of the 'Get Rich Quick' ad in the paper also involves what I call TABU Tales, which brings us on to our next myth.

Myth #2: Magic Marketing And TABU Tales

Some people litter the internet with ads that run along these lines: 'Sign up to learn my advanced online marketing secrets and you'll be a millionaire before you know it.'

If you respond to the ad, you will *not* just receive a letter (or an email) telling you to run ads offering online marketing secrets. The game has grown a little more sophisticated since those early days of GRQ ads in the paper. What you will receive, in typical cases, is an impressive bundle of materials outlining the secrets of super smart online marketing: a glossy 'welcome' booklet featuring professional models looking smug and rich, a step-by-step workbook to follow, access to some 'inner sanctum' training videos and so on. It's easy to imagine that if you just follow your golden guru's advice, you will soon be enjoying the wealth you so keenly desire.

Sadly, this is unlikely to happen. Let me explain why. In his book 'Fast 800', Dr. Michael Mosley talks about useless advice. He gives the example of a tennis coach who promises he can tell aspiring players how to win matches and tournaments. When tennis enthusiasts sign up, he gives them this advice: win more points than your opponent. You can't say the advice isn't accurate. If you win more points, you *will* win matches. The problem is that it misses out the part that matters: *how* to win more points. I refer to this type of advice as a TABU tale: Technically Accurate But Useless.

In my opinion, and in my experience, some of the gurus who advertise their amazing marketing know-how are simply offering TABU Tales. When you analyse their material, it boils down to this:

First, have a really great idea for a product: one that lots of people will be really keen to buy; one that really makes a big difference to the lives of thousands or even millions of people. A 'killer' product that the world will adore.

Then, advertise it online to drive people to your website where you have set up landing pages and a sales funnel.

We're back to 'win more points than your opponent'. I'm sure that if you come up with a brilliant product that lots of people want to buy, you will probably make a lot of money. On this, we can all agree. The question is, how do you do this? Dreaming up this kind of world-beating, must-have product is extremely difficult — so difficult, in fact, that it only happens a few times per generation.

What's more, if you're trying to come up with something that will make life better for large numbers of people, you're competing with the research and development teams of every massive multi-national company in the world. Good luck with that.

TABU Tales are all over the internet. There's no shortage of programs, courses, videos, seminars and conferences dangling the lure of easy wealth. However, what's actually on offer is often just another TABU Tale in a fancy costume: come up with a great idea that everyone will love. How could it be otherwise? What did you think your marketing guru was going to offer? A goose that lays golden eggs?

When I described the 'Get Rich Quick' newspaper scam, I asked you note two points. (1) The seller has nothing to offer except the idea of making money by saying they know to make money. (2) Secondly, there's no exchange of value. Whenever you encounter an ad that runs along the lines of 'get rich by learning my super marketing secrets', see if these two points apply. What does this guru or teacher actually *know* about, or know how to *do*, other than running ads about making money? What's their skill set or talent apart from running GRQ ads? Secondly, where's the exchange of value? Is there really anything on offer apart from advice that says, 'the way to get rich is to have an idea that will make you rich'. I'm not seeing a lot of value in this.

By the way, I don't mean to be grouchy about all this. I do understand the lure of GRQ ads and TABU Tales, in all their rich variety. I can even admire the glossy sophistication of some GRQ operations and how they re-invent themselves for each new generation. I know that in a free market economy people can offer and buy whatever they want. If Jack wants to set up the WMP Tennis Academy (it stands for 'Win More Points') and Jill signs up for it, that's their business and their transaction. Maybe they'll both have some fun.

All I'm saying is, by all means strive to be successful but please don't spend too much time, or money you can't afford, chasing golden unicorns. You have better things to do.

One final note. Nothing in this section is about legitimate digital marketing firms and consultancies. They do *not* spout empty 'get rich quick' nonsense. They *do* offer specialist know-how and expertise in what can be a complex and rapidly evolving arena; they work hard for their clients to devise realistic marketing plans, involving plenty of sustained effort; and they often provide excellent value. No crazy promises or unicorns. Please bear this distinction in mind.

Myth #3: Big Numbers

It's easy to get the impression that success is about big numbers and exclamation marks. This is especially true if you happen to be a performer or do anything creative. The media *love* big numbers and never tire of reporting them in a rather excitable manner.

'This book has sold over a million copies!'

'This movie grossed eleventy gazillion dollars in its first week!'

'On this singer's last tour, she sold more tickets than the entire population of the world multiplied by seven!"

Big numbers often owe more to a publicist's imagination than reality. However, even when they are accurate, all they can do is tell you something about *popularity,* which can be cruelly fickle and fleeting. They do not tell you anything about *success.*

Maybe that book was actually terrible and the author made very little money after their publisher and the retailers had taken their share. Maybe that movie was subsequently judged to be awful and everyone in it struggled to find work afterwards. Maybe that singer has a terrible life, is very unhappy and will soon spiral out of control. Who knows?

You can understand why publicists focus on big numbers. They sound impressive (if you don't think about them too much) and make for easy headlines and neat soundbites. I'm just saying that big numbers, alluring as they may be, have little if anything to do with *success.*

Myth #4: Celebrity Culture

Success has nothing to do with the bright lights and tinsel of celebrity culture. In case it's not immediately obvious, celebrity culture is about one thing: luring people towards advertising. That's the only purpose it serves and the only purpose it *can* serve.

Hey, let's watch this TV coverage of a movie premiere. We know the movie is important because we've been told it is. Look, there's an actress we recognise. She's smiling at everyone and being given the full 'red carpet' treatment. Some people are taking her photograph and someone else is going to interview her. Her hair looks nice and she's wearing a glamorous frock.

Why is all this happening? You don't have to be a genius to figure it out. The actress is there to deliver a commercial benefit to a few different companies. Obviously, she's there to encourage you to see the movie itself, thereby helping the studio to turn a profit. She also happens to be standing in front of several corporate sponsor logos. What about that beautiful, gorgeous dress? She's wearing it so that the brand or designer gets a mention. The photographs that are being taken will end up in the press and on websites to lure your eyes and your mind to adverts. The TV channel you're watching is hoping to win your attention long enough to fire some ads into your brain. You are part of the statistics on their 'rates and data' card they show to advertisers.

To the extent that this actress serves the needs of these commercial interests, she will continue to feature in the media. So long as someone, somewhere, figures she can assist their corporate interests and help to keep the shareholders happy, she will continue to enjoy a touch of fame. As soon as she is deemed to no longer deliver the desired commercial advantage, she will be dropped and the media will focus on someone else. If you want, you can read accounts by former 'celebrities' in various fields, not just the acting profession, of what life is like once the corporate interests transfer their favours elsewhere.

This isn't a *cynical* attitude. It's just a healthily *realistic* one. All I'm saying is that unless you have a *very* strange understanding of the word 'success', you can't measure it in terms of how well you serve as bait for washing powder commercials. John Updike famously described fame as 'the mask that eats away the face', which I think sums it up rather well.

(Technical note: I know some people advocate using 'actor' as a gender-neutral term. My friend Abbie is a highly talented professional thespian and tells me she prefers the term 'actress'. She's my friend so that's the term I use.)

168

A Crippling Disease

Just before I close this section, I want to share my views about 'celebrity culture'. This isn't *strictly* relevant to this book, so you can skip this part if you want, but I'd just like to place my opinion on record.

I don't like celebrity culture. In fact I despise it and see it as a disfiguring disease that our species tragically inflicts on itself. It is the crass and ugly graffiti that we spray over the beauty of our spirit and the majesty of our potential. Celebrity culture says this:

> Here's a very small group of people. They may be singers, comedians, actors, models, authors, sports people, pundits or people who run a successful business. This small group of people is worthy of your attention. They are worth writing about in magazines, inviting on to chat shows, being given a stage and some bright lights. They deserve to be interviewed and are worthy of comment in gossip rags and on celebrity story-scraper websites.

> The rest of you? Pah! You're nothing. You're not interesting or worthy of any attention. Your role is just to be passive, silent, unimportant workers and consumers. Your role is to sit and watch these people that are deemed worthy of attention. It's important that you do this because it enables someone, somewhere (but not you) to make money and turn a profit.

I heartily reject this attitude.

I love people more than this. I love people enough to know that everyone deserves my time and attention. I know that everyone has their story and that if I listen to them I'll hear amazing things: surprises, joys, disappointments, tough times and heroic triumphs, all the stuff and unfathomably chaotic richness of a precious, fascinating human life. I say that everyone, and every life, is worth celebrating.

I could turn on the TV (if I had one) and watch someone appear on a chat show to promote their latest product. For some reason, this just doesn't interest me. I'd prefer to hang out with my friends because they're far more interesting and entertaining than anyone I've ever seen on a chat show.

I'd rather chat to the receptionist at the hotel, the manager of the coffee shop, the shelf-stacker in the supermarket, the guy washing cars for a living, the street sweeper and the farmer worried about the market price for milk. I'd rather connect with real people and real lives. There is so much to love and admire in people and so many smiles to share.

To be clear, I don't despise any of the celebrities who enjoy their moments or years in the limelight. What I despise is the mad machinery that can surround and infect them, presenting a dishonest and insulting demarcation between 'interesting' people and the rest. Whenever I see a chat show on TV, I look at the people in the audience. I feel sure that each and every one of them would be just as interesting, just as worthy of being interviewed, as the guests on the show.

Celebrity culture is flawed. It says that one tiny group of people are worth paying attention to. It doesn't celebrate humanity. It spits at it, or well over 99% of it, and declares, "Sorry, you're not among the important, beautiful and interesting people who are worthy of attention, so sit down, shut up and watch in silence."

I reject celebrity culture because I don't think, "You don't matter much" is a good message to send out to people via every channel and website. To my mind, we need a lot more of the opposite message: "I believe in you. You matter. I'm fascinated by your story and your potential, and you should be too because there's only one of you and you're amazing."

You turn on the TV and a presenter introduces someone who has a new song to promote. So what? Why not turn off the TV and make up your own song? It's more fun — in fact, the less musical talent you have the more fun it can be! At least you'll actually be *doing* something rather than just watching someone else who you are told, quite arbitrarily, is worth watching.

No matter who you are, I believe in you. I don't believe your only role in this world is to sit, mute and passive, watching other people that a producer has arbitrarily deemed to be interesting. I'd rather listen to your story, hear your dreams and aspirations, have a laugh, hear your pain and the lessons you've learned, buy you a coffee and connect with you. You are the celebrity. You are the star of your life and as far as I'm concerned it's the greatest show on earth.

* * *

What's Next?

Having looked at success mythology, it's time to move on to success reality — including a slight improvement on the notion of 'positive thinking' .

18. Success Reality

"I'm sick of following my dreams. I'm just going to ask them where they're going and hook up with them later."

— Mitch Hedberg

18. Success Reality

In the previous chapter, we looked at various aspects of success mythology. Now we can move on to look at success reality.

Defining Success

You can't pursue what you can't define, so what exactly do we mean by 'success'? Everyone has their preferred definition and here's mine:

Success is fulfilling your potential, whatever that happens to be.

In my view, your fundamental purpose in life, insofar as you have one, is to fulfil your potential and, in doing so, help others to do the same.

You don't get to choose your potential (they say Mozart could compose symphonies when he was eight). You *do* get to choose how much of your potential you fulfil, or at least how close you get by virtue of your own efforts. Luck and circumstance play a part, of course, but they are irrelevant to your success story. Bad luck isn't your fault so you can't be blamed for it. Good luck isn't an achievement so you can't claim credit for it — unless you want to be an example of survivorship bias.

What matters is working to get as close as you can to fulfilling your potential, and the sense of honest pride, satisfaction and joy you get in the process. How you translate this general principle into the reality of your self-employment journey is, of course, entirely up to you. Maybe you're going to be a great entertainer, build a ceramics factory, open a pet grooming salon, invent a better potato peeler, build skyscrapers or run the friendliest cake shop in town. Only you know what 'fulfilling your potential' means to you and therefore what your personal version of 'success' will look like.

There's another definition of success that I'd also like to share with you:

Success is the name we give to a story of time and effort, trial and error, talent, mistakes and problems, plus a bit of luck, that somehow ends up in a good place.

Success can take many forms but it's seldom a neat story or a straight path. If you read a few honest biographies of 'successful' people you'll soon realise there tends to be quite a lot of chaos involved!

All that said, assuming you want to be successful, how should you go about it?

Step 1. Believe In Yourself x 4

A lot of books about success say a good starting point is for you to believe in yourself. I wholeheartedly agree. Positive self-belief is an excellent launch pad for success. In fact, I suggest you break this general principle down into four points.

Believe in **yourself and your potential**. Everybody is different from you but nobody is *better* than you. You're great, with amazing potential to fulfil. You have a contribution to make and only you can make it. Nobody else can make it for you.

Believe in your **value**. You're unique so you have a unique contribution to make, a unique offer to make to the world. The world won't always be very appreciative but that's the world's problem, not yours.

Believe in your **work**. If it makes sense to you, then it's worth doing. When you start out, it isn't anyone else's job to believe in your product, your work or your vision. It's *your* job so enjoy doing it. It's okay if it takes the rest of the world a little time to catch up with you.

Believe in your **entitlement to rewards**. The benefit you get from fulfilling your potential will vary. You might want material wealth or just satisfied customers and enough money to get by, doing something you love. Regardless of the specifics, believe you are entitled to rewards of many kinds: financial, emotional and personal.

The Two Sweepers

Here's a story that features in many business books and 'motivational' talks.

A young man has a rather menial job sweeping the streets. One day, he sees someone drive by in a beautiful, luxury limousine. It's a stunning piece of engineering and he is filled with dismay and envy. He sighs wistfully, allowing himself a moment of self-pity. "Life's so unfair," he thinks, sadly shaking his head. "Why can't I have a car like that?"

In another part of town, there's another young man who is also sweeping the streets. As it happens, he sees the same beautiful car. He takes a moment to admire the car as it passes by. "Wow!" he says. "That's the most impressive car I've ever seen. One day, I'm going to have a car just like that!"

Same experience but a very different attitude. Believe in your entitlement to rewards and your ability to work towards obtaining them.

Step 2. Have A Clear Goal

You can't aim the arrow unless you know where the target is. You can't plan the journey unless you know the destination. You can't deliver the package unless you know the address.

All these metaphors (and I could dream up a few more) are a way to make the same point: you have to have a clear goal in mind or else your efforts will, by definition, be aimless.

Whatever goal you intend to pursue, it has to have two qualities. First of all, it has to be ambitious. You have to 'think big'. Why? A better question would be: why not? For one thing, it's a lot more fun. For another, big ambitions have more power to inspire you and to inspire others. Secondly, your goal must also be realistic. If your goal is to eat your own head or run a mile in ten seconds, I can save you some time and trouble: you're not going to get there. Take some time out for a reality check and a re-think.

Some people feel there's a contradiction between being ambitious and being realistic. There isn't. Being ambitious does not mean dreaming up crazy, fantastical notions that will obviously never come true. It means aiming high but aiming at a target you can actually hit.

It's okay for your goal to evolve over time, in the light of experience. In fact, it would be unusual if it did not. I've revised my own goals and ambitions many times over the past twenty years. However, when you start off, you have to have a clear destination in mind or else you can't plan how to get there.

Step 3. Pursue One Main Goal

Here's a simple exercise to try. Hold up a finger, more or less directly in front of you. Move it to the left. That was pretty easy, wasn't it? Start again, once more holding your finger in front of yourself. Move it to the right. Also very easy to do.

Start again and this time try to move your finger both left and right *at the same time*. You can't do it, can you? It's impossible. You take two things, both of which seem perfectly easy, but when you put them together you suddenly can't achieve either of them. You're frozen, stalled, unable to make any progress.

This may seem stunningly obvious yet it's not quite as obvious as you might think. Many people who start working for themselves are like someone trying to move both left and right at the same time. They stretch themselves in many different directions and fail to focus on one main goal. As a result, they don't actually make any progress towards anything. This is a good way to squander a lot of time and effort so you end up feeling rather frustrated.

It's okay if you have one main goal and a few smaller side projects that don't interfere with your progress. It's okay if your main goal evolves over time and you make slight corrections to your course. What doesn't work is trying to pursue incompatible or conflicting goals at the same time. Clarity of purpose is your friend.

Step 4. Focus Mostly On Effort

The next step is to consider the ingredients of success. There are four parts to any success story: talent, time, luck and effort. One of these things is not like the others.

You don't have much control over your natural talents and aptitudes. They are just whatever you're born with. It's true that if you have a particular talent you can work to make the most of it, but you can't improve what isn't there.

You also don't have much control over time. We all tend to get the same allocation (about 24 hours per day). What you can do is strive to make the best *use* of the time you have available. I suspect not many success stories feature dozing in bed until noon, watching soap operas or playing video games all day.

You don't have any control over luck. By definition, luck is what you can't control. You can, however, try to create as many opportunities as possible for luck to come your way. As a wise person once said, "Chance favours the prepared mind".

The part that you have *total* control over is the effort. You can decide how much effort you make and how consistently. You can make the effort to exercise, keep in good shape and be careful what you eat. You can make the effort to develop your talent and knowledge. You can make the effort to be organised and dependable so that you don't let people down. You can make the effort to provide the best products or services you possibly can. You can make the effort to find your market and get the word out.

I suggest you don't waste too much time worrying about the things you can't do much about: the talent, time and luck. Focus mostly on the part you can control: the effort. Work hard, work smart and work consistently towards your fulfilment.

Step 5. Spot Opportunities, Take Action

There's one point that every success guru in the world tends to mention: we are all swimming in a sea of opportunities all the time. Successful people tend to notice these opportunities, other people don't.

Here's a story that features in a lot of business books. A shoe salesman goes to a distant, tropical country to assess the market. He finds that everyone goes around in bare feet. He sends a message back to head office: "Complete waste of time. No market, nobody here wears shoes." Shortly after, a rival salesman visits the same place. Rather excitedly, he sends a message back to head office: "Amazing luck! Send all stock you can! Massive new market — nobody here wears shoes yet!"

Stay alert and notice the opportunities that come your way. In fact, you can *prime* your mind to notice opportunities that you might otherwise miss. Ordinarily, you aren't aware how many red cars you see on a given day. However, if one morning you tell yourself to spot three red cars during the day, you will. It's the same with opportunities. At the start of the week, meditate and tell your mind you want to notice three interesting opportunities this week. You'll spot them!

Having noticed an opportunity, the next important part is to *act* on it. There are two elements to this. The first is to act fairly promptly. In many cases, the window of opportunity doesn't stay open for very long. I am *not* suggesting you act either impulsively or recklessly. You can respond to opportunities promptly yet still be cautious and thoughtful. Secondly, you may need to be persistent. If an opportunity involves knocking on a door, don't be surprised if you have to knock a few times before it opens. If you can be persistent while always remaining polite, patient, respectful and friendly, you'll find most of the doors open eventually.

The Art Of Avoiding Regret

There's one more point I want to add about opportunities.

When I was at school, I was offered the chance to sit the Oxbridge entrance exam, the first step to getting a place at either Oxford or Cambridge University. It was clear this would involve a lot of extra work and I wasn't sure I wanted to try for it, especially as I'd heard that there were thirty-five applicants for every place. I discussed it with my mother. She said, "You have to do it. If you don't, you'll spend the rest of your life wondering what would have happened if you had."

I did the extra work and sat the exam. Not surprisingly, I didn't get selected. In one sense, it's possible to see this as a waste of time.

However, it led to some interesting experiences and, looking back, I'm glad I tried.

When an opportunity comes along, the point is not necessarily whether it will lead to major success. Sometimes, the point is that you'll have the experience and the memory of having tried rather than the regret of wondering what *would* have happened if you *had* tried.

Before moving on, I need to add a small note. As I've just mentioned, I was never accepted as a student at either Oxford or Cambridge. However, a few years ago the Oxford University Scientific Society invited me to give a lecture about psychic phenomena. Not long after that, one of the Cambridge colleges invited me to present a special lecture about achieving impossible goals (something I lecture on now and again). So while it's true that neither of these magnificent palaces of higher learning ever wanted me as a student, I have been invited to *lecture* at *both* of them! I'll take this as a partial win for me.

Now I just have to wait for the calls from Harvard and Yale.

Step 6. Prefer Positive Doing

A lot of success gurus focus on positive thinking. Norman Vincent Peale started it all with his splendid book, 'The Power of Positive Thinking', first published in 1952 and still sell well.

I'm all for a bit of positive thinking but I suggest to my private students that they prefer positive *doing* instead. It's like positive thinking except you get things done. In my view, doing is much better than wondering and speculating.

There's no point just endlessly speculating about what would happen if you tried to be a rap singer or photographer, or if you opened a small retail business, or became a hypnotherapist, or started a new online business exporting surgical stockings to Lithuania. It's far better to actually try it and see.

Discover by doing, learn by living. One grain of experience is worth ten buckets of idle speculation. What's more, you'll find that trying something — even if you find you're not very good at it — tends to open doors and paths towards the things you *are* good at. Speculation achieves little. To *do* is to *discover*.

Positive thinking is fine as far as it goes, but positive doing gets more done, is more fun, teaches you more and makes the right impression on other people.

Step 7. Be Ready For Breaks

If you start working for yourself and doing your own thing, you will occasionally get a 'break' of some kind: a significant opportunity that could make a big difference to your success. This can take many forms. It could be the chance to win a big order from a new customer, to get on the books of a good agency or get a series of gigs that will allow you to build up lots of experience.

The only certain thing about breaks is their uncertainty. You never know when they will come along and they are inherently unpredictable. The point is that when a break *does* come along, you have to be ready for it. Ready to impress. Ready to show that you can deliver the goods.

A Sad Scenario

There's a very sad scenario that I've seen played out countless times. Imagine a keen young singer called Jill. She tries hard, knocks on doors, pursues her dream. Finally, she gets five minutes to audition for someone who could make a big difference to her career. "Go ahead, show me what you can do," says this powerful, influential person.

Jill turns in a terrible performance. She lets herself down and doesn't deliver the goods. The golden opportunity is wasted. She might say, "It was an off day, I was nervous, just give me one more chance." Frankly, she can say whatever she wants because it won't make any difference. The chance has gone.

I've seen this kind of thing happen many times. While it's true that anyone can have a bad day, the point is to be as prepared as possible to capitalise on whatever breaks come your way. Always be ready to make your case, explain your vision, deliver the goods, strut your stuff and make a good impression.

Step 8. Be Persistent

A lot of success books and experts extol the virtues of tenacity and persistence. They may offer quotes like this:

> "Nothing in this world can take the place of persistence. Talent will not; nothing is more common than unsuccessful people with talent. Genius will not; unrewarded genius is almost a proverb. Education will not; the world is full of educated derelicts. Persistence and determination alone are omnipotent."
> — Calvin Coolidge

This is fine for the 'easy soundbite' school of business wisdom. However, for anyone who prefers to live in the real world, it's not quite as simple as that. The truth is that persistence comes in two very different flavours: admirable and foolish.

Persistence is admirable when you have a good idea and you see it through, thereby realising its full potential. It means you deal with problems and don't let them throw you off course. You may get knocked down a few times but you smile, get back up and carry on. Every success story you've ever heard of involved numerous setbacks, stumbles, mistakes, bad luck and rotten days. This is why persistence is vital.

Persistence is foolish when you have a bad idea and you see it through regardless, even though there's plenty of evidence *telling* you it's a bad idea.

How do you tell the difference? Well, in terms of your artistic success, I'm not sure. Perhaps there's no easy way to tell them apart. After all, many successful artistic ventures get off to a disappointing start.

In terms of your *commercial* success, it's much easier to distinguish between admirable and foolish persistence. How much interest is there in your product? How much money are you making? What does your bank account look like? Are you getting good reactions and do people want to pay for your product or service? It's true that it can take a while to establish a new business and get some money coming in. However, the evidence is usually pretty clear to anyone who isn't willingly blind to it.

If you want to be a singer but nobody wants to pay to hear you sing, then the best favour you can do yourself is to realise you haven't got a commercially viable proposition. You can sing all you want for your artistic fulfilment. Sing for free at parties, sing in a field, sing in the street, have fun. In the meantime you'll need to get a job or do something else to pay for food.

How long do you wait before you decide whether your persistence is admirable or foolish? This is obviously a judgment call that only you can make for yourself, but I can offer you a pretty good clue. If you're staring into a financial abyss, then (a) it's foolish persistence and (b) you should have realised this sooner.

Admirable persistence: good. Foolish persistence: bad.

Try not to get them mixed up!

Step 9. Smile, Get Up Again

When you work for yourself, I can guarantee you'll get knocked down a few times. This is as sure as the sunrise. You will face indifference and unfair criticism. People will sometimes hurt your feelings. There will be times when you make a complete mess of things. You will fail and stumble and life's fundamental unfairness will often confound you.

Fortunately, you have a magical power over all these things that renders them unable to prevent your eventual success. Here it is: smile and get up again. That's it. That's your magical power. It renders all the stumbles and setbacks powerless to stop you or get in your way.

So you get knocked down? Smile. Get up again. Learn from it and carry on (while always remembering the difference between admirable and foolish persistence).

Step 10. Always Learn From Experience

Experience will teach you how to be successful if you allow it to. There are only two ways in which this can go wrong.

One is if you never actually try or do anything. You can't learn from experience you haven't had. The second is to ignore the lessons that experience is trying to teach you. This is where an awareness of bad or unhealthy persistence is a great thing to have. If there's no money coming in, if absolutely nobody wants what you're selling, if you do ten comedy gigs and nobody laughs even once, then there comes a point when you have to listen to what experience is trying to tell you. This may mean significantly changing your plans.

I've heard stories of people who feel they were let down by other people, or by rotten luck and bad timing. I've also heard stories of people who felt they let themselves down. However, I have never heard of people being let down by experience and the lessons it taught them.

* * *

What's Next?

The next section offers a few additional thoughts on success, including an intriguing new book by the popular singer Madonna. Surprisingly, it's all about gardening!

19. Further Thoughts On Success

"I'm also good at meditation. It involves doing nothing and everything at the same time."

— Mike Oldfield

19. Further Thoughts On Success

The previous chapter listed some good steps to take if you want to be successful. Here are a few further thoughts on success.

About Competition

Don't worry about competition. This is not your job. Your job is to be as good as you can be at whatever you do, maximise every opportunity, fulfil your potential and have a great life.

The people who do the same sort of thing as you will basically fall into three groups. There will be some who aren't quite as good as you. When you see their work, they remind you how good you are. This is a nice little stroke for your ego. There will be some who are equally as good as you. It's better to be friends, or friendly rivals, with these people than to think of one another as enemies. Peer group respect is a wonderful thing to enjoy. Finally, there will be some people you feel are actually better than you. Regard them as inspiration and motivation, as these are the only people you can learn from. They might be better than you today but tomorrow is always another story. Watch, learn and admire them but don't try to *be* them or to copy them.

You'll find that the majority of self-employed people have a very co-operative spirit. They take the view that there's plenty of work to go round for people who are any good, we all collectively help to grow the market and there's no need to regard one another as a threat. It's good to be competitive, in the sense of trying to be the best you can be, but this doesn't mean you can't be friends with other players in the same market and build constructive relationships with them.

Originality Versus Similarity

If you are an entertainer, the subject of competition raises an interesting point. Should you aim to be highly original and distinctive? Or do you give the market what it wants, which necessarily means being quite similar to what's already out there?

First of all, unless you're a tribute act, never try to copy another act or another performer. It won't work, it's unethical and it's never going to be fulfilling. The best you'll ever be is a pale copy of someone else, rather than yourself.

Beyond that, you have two paths to success.

You can present something new, original and distinctive that the market doesn't know it wants yet. This means you have to do all the hard work of convincing the market that, although you're unfamiliar and different, they'll like you if they give you a chance.

Alternatively, you can present something pretty similar to acts that the market already approves of. This is an easier sell but you'll never be regarded as very special. Nobody's going to say you were a 'game changer'. Maybe you can live without this ego stroke.

The Difficult Second Album Syndrome

These points about originality bring to mind a well-known phenomenon in the music industry: the 'difficult second album' syndrome. Imagine a young, ambitious rock band. They get signed to a record label and put out their first album. They enjoy a bit of success, appear on all the music shows, do interviews and go on tour.

After a while, it's time for the band to release their second album. The problem is that whatever they do, they're in for a critical mauling. If the second album is similar to the first, the music journalists can be nasty and say:

> "The new effort from Band X is scarcely new at all, being little more than a re-tread of their debut album. There are few signs of fresh inspiration and it seems they used up all their good ideas the first time around. How could they run out of steam so quickly?"

If the second album is very different from the first, the music journalists can be unkind in a different way:

> "The new effort from Band X is, sadly, a far cry from the glories of their debut. It seems they've quickly forgotten everything that made us like them in the first place. Clearly incapable of recapturing the joys of their first offering, they've instead opted to dabble in a confusing mish-mash of styles that is distinctly lacking. A friendly word of advice to them: if it ain't broke, don't fix it."

Markets can be perverse and elusive. If you offer novelty, people may say they prefer the comfort of the familiar. If you offer what's familiar, people may say they want something new. When it comes to creative and artistic endeavours, there are no rules or guarantees. There are only efforts and results. Try your best, throw the dice, see where they fall and have great stories to tell your grandchildren.

Pride Versus Profit

As I have mentioned elsewhere in this book, there is artistic success and commercial success. Artistic success means you create art that you're proud of. Commercial success means you can buy food.

It's very helpful to avoid confusing these two notions. Artistic success is great but if you try using it to buy a loaf of bread you won't get very far. This is why, earlier in this book, I suggested you should fall in love with commercial reality. Nonetheless, you can be very proud of your work even if it doesn't sell and you should be. There's always something to admire about being active and creative, even if the result doesn't exactly catapult you into a world of limitless wealth.

Some years ago, I wrote a book of original romantic poetry called 'The Moon Carrier'. This was an ambitious project that involved collaborating with an illustrator for about eighteen months. I also invested quite a lot of money in the project. Hardly anyone wanted to buy this book and I sold very few copies. In terms of commercial viability, it was right up there with the pen sharpener and knitted diving boots.

Nonetheless, I am fiercely proud of that book! I had a very specific idea in my mind about how I wanted it to look and I worked hard to turn my idea into reality. It didn't make money but it wasn't meant to. It's just something I felt I wanted to create so I created it.

The Truth About Talent

Being talented means you can do something to a fairly high standard. Let me add a note about this.

If doesn't matter whether you think you're good at something or what your family and friends say. When complete strangers say you're good at something, that's when you know you're good at it. When they say it often enough, and pay you well enough, that you enjoy a nice standard of living, that's when you know you're really good at it — at least in terms of your commercial success.

Self-belief is great and essential to your success. However, self-delusion is pointless and very damaging to your success. This doesn't just apply to artists, performers and entertainers. It's the same in the world of business and trade. You might think you're a great florist, carpet-fitter or butcher but the market's verdict is what counts.

If you want to know if you're good at what you do, I suggest you take a look at your bank balance. I promise it won't lie to you.

The Madonna Gardening Book Theory

During the early days of your journey into self-employment, you may be tempted to impress the world with your remarkable versatility. This is especially true if you're a performer or entertainer. You may want everyone to know that you do comedy, but you're also a fine actor, you can juggle, you design ornamental candles, you can play bass trombone and you're brilliant at furniture restoration.

Don't do this. It just leads to confusion about who you are and what you do. You will lack a clear, well defined identity so people won't know which category you belong in or how to use you. Instead, focus on one thing you do really well and let this define you. It might be hard to resist mentioning all your other brilliant talents but do your best to shut up about them unless you're asked.

Offer a clear identity to the market. Make it easy for people to know if they can use you. When you have enjoyed some success, when you're getting regular work and earning good money, *then* it's okay to mention that you do other things and branch out a bit.

Suppose Madonna wrote a book about gardening tips. Any publishing company would love to publish her book and it would probably sell very well. However, this is only true because Madonna has spent decades establishing her reputation as one of the most successful pop singers in the world. Not a pop singer, juggler, lion tamer, stilt-walker, chef and watercolour artist.

Success Takes Many Forms

In the earlier section on Success Mythology, I mentioned the media's obsession with big numbers that leads to a very narrow and distorted view of success. You're only a successful writer if you've had several 'Top Ten Bestseller' books. You're only a successful singer if you've had a number one album and sold millions of tickets on tour. You're only a successful businessman if you've got a vast personal fortune and a private island with gold-plated bath taps and a helipad.

This is all simplistic nonsense. Success takes many forms.

I think I'm entitled to regard myself as a reasonably successful writer. I'm not claiming to have written best-selling books that have made me rich and famous. What I *can* say is that for thirty years or so, I've been able to earn a decent living as a freelance writer. I've done something I love, I've been fairly well paid for it and I've fulfilled most of my dreams, such as travelling all over the world and having a lot of fun.

My friend Adam Bloom is a brilliant and very successful comedian. He hasn't become a darling of the media, doesn't turn up on every chat show and panel game and hasn't so far sold out a string of top arenas (although he does play some major venues). What he *has* done, for over twenty years, is made a lot of people laugh all over the world, been well paid for it and enjoyed a pretty high standard of living.

My friend Joshua Paxton is a world-class jazz pianist. He isn't rich or famous and often plays in bars and clubs to earn a bit of money. He's as happy and content as anyone I know. He takes this view: "Every day I don't go into an office, it's another win, another day of success for me."

I could provide many other examples. My point is that the version of 'success' served up by some sections of the mass media is very narrow and misleading. Don't get taken in by it.

If You Want A Guarantee, Get A Toaster

If you buy a toaster, you usually get a guarantee with it. The manufacturer includes a piece of paper saying that if the device happens to spontaneously explode one morning, incinerating your home, leaving everyone with sooty faces, scaring the cat and otherwise delivering a seriously deficient toasting experience, you can get your money back.

Toasters come with guarantees but, unfortunately, not everything else does. Life doesn't and neither does working for yourself. It's possible to put in all the hard work, do everything right and still end up nowhere. This is true whether you get a normal job or decide to run your own business.

Self-employed people understand this. We take the view that it's better to try to lead a fulfilled life, even if we fail, then to never even try and spend our lives doing things for other people. In reality, the only failure is not to try.

That having been said, complete failure is extremely rare. I know a great many people, all over the world, who work for themselves. In the past twenty years, I think I've heard of precisely one person whose decision to pursue self-employment just didn't work out. In the end, he went back to doing the same office job he'd done before. I talked to him not so long ago and he doesn't seem too unhappy about it. He's glad that he tried, even if he didn't enjoy a great deal of success.

If you decide to work for yourself, you may fall short of your early goals and dreams. However, you'll probably still find a way to survive, get by and to have some sort of a fulfilled life.

186

While there are no guarantees, I think a life where you strive to fulfil your potential, see where your talents and efforts can take you, and have all the adventures that are yours to have, is a great life. Even if you only achieve half of what you hoped for, it's still going to be worth it.

Personally, I'd prefer that to being stuck in an office, bored out of my mind, getting to 65 and realising I've got a head full of dead ambitions and a heart full of regrets that go, "I wonder what would have happened if…"

* * *

What's Next?

The next section is about motivation. Among other things, you'll meet a talking rabbit and a problem with two tables!

20. Thoughts To Share

"I have dreamed in my life dreams that have stayed with me ever after, and changed my ideas; they have gone through and through me, like wine through water, and altered the colour of my mind."

— Emily Brontë

20. Thoughts To Share

I don't see myself as being in the motivation business. Nonetheless, if people ask me for a little of the 'motivational' stuff, here are the three ideas I usually share.

Inspiration #1: Your 'It's Too Late' Day

I remember once sitting with my elderly father towards the end of his life. He was in pretty good health for his age but he was frail and weak. Even getting around his own home was something of a challenge.

There was a documentary on TV and it included a few shots of New York. He said to me, "You know, I always wanted to go to New York and see it for myself."

I asked him why. "Oh, nothing specific," he replied. "It just always looked so interesting and full of things I'd like to see." Then he added these simple words: "Of course, it's too late now."

No matter how well you look after yourself, sooner or later your body will start to let you down, or your mind will, or both. When this happens, your options start being taken away from you. The day will come when any unfulfilled ambitions you have are going to stay unfulfilled. There are no second chances and there's nothing you can do about it. This is your 'It's too late' day.

There's no getting away from it: your 'It's too late' day is coming. Here are some suggestions.

If there are things you want to do, do them. If there are things you want to try, try them. If there are things you want to see and places you want to visit, go to see them and visit them. If there are people you want to meet, go to meet them.

Of course, life doesn't always accommodate every wish and your plans can be thwarted. My suggestions still stand. If there are a hundred things you want to do, it's better to have done ninety of them than only ten.

Live your life in such a way that you'll never have much cause to say, "It's too late now."

Aim instead for this sort of feeling: "I pretty much did everything I wanted to do, tried everything I wanted to try and went everywhere I wanted to go. Yep, it's been great!"

190

Inspiration #2: The One Way Wall

A few years ago I visited the Berlin Wall, or at least the memorial based around what's left of it. It is, of course, a poignant and thought-provoking place to visit.

The American writer and humourist P. J. O'Rourke, in his 1992 book 'Give War A Chance', wrote a darkly witty account of the fall of the Berlin Wall and all it represented. One of O'Rourke's themes in his article is that we don't need to wonder which side won the Cold War or had the superior ideology. He points out that large numbers of people tried to escape from the East to the West but none ever desired to go the other way. This, O'Rourke concludes, tells us all we need to know.

I see a parallel with how I feel about the self-employed way of life versus the alternative. I apologise in advance if you feel this is rather glib and disrespectful to the very sombre history of the Berlin Wall.

Over the past twenty years, I have had more conversations than I can count with people who have a regular, nine-to-five job but say they would desperately love to give it up and work for themselves. This is a conversation I've had all over the world with many different people, young and old. Almost all of them actually use the verb 'escape'. I have literally never had a conversation with anyone, anywhere, who wanted to go the other way.

A point that I make several times in this book is that there is nothing easy about working for yourself and running your own business. I maintain that however you analyse it, and whichever list of pros and cons you draw up, the equation comes out the same way: if you want an easy life, get a job in an office, sit in your cubicle and do what you're told. Just hope they miss your name in the next, grimly inevitable round of 'organisational restructuring'.

I know vast numbers of self-employed people. I don't know a single one who thinks they have an easy life. What they do have is a *fulfilled* life, a sense of honouring their own spirit, their desire to see where their own skills, talents and wits can take them, whether this leads to rainbows and champagne or thistles and bruises.

What should we conclude from this? I don't know but I will offer this suggestion: maybe you're reading this book, at this point in your life, for a reason. Think about it.

Also, think about the fact that nobody will ever write a book about how to escape from the self-employed side of life into Office Land. Nor would anyone ever want to read it.

Inspiration #3: The Two Tables

You'll have to use a little imagination for this.

A White Rabbit is giving a talk and you're in the audience. The Rabbit is standing between two tables.

On Table 1 are lots of gift-wrapped boxes with appealing labels such as 'Good health', 'A loving relationship', 'Wealth', 'Good times'.

On Table 2 are boxes with less appealing labels: 'Average or poor health', 'No relationship', 'Never enough money', 'Boredom'.

The White Rabbit invites a woman from the audience to come to the front. "Congratulations!" says the Rabbit while pointing to Table 1, "You can have all these things!" The woman scoops up all the boxes in her arms and walks off to claps and cheers. (The boxes are instantly replaced.)

The Rabbit invites someone else to come up. He, too, is awarded all the boxes on Table 1. Everyone claps and the man walks off looking pleased.

Eventually, it's your turn. You come forward and the Rabbit says, "Sorry, you can't have anything on Table 1. However, take anything you want from Table 2."

You feel annoyed. "But I want those nice things on Table 1!"

"Sorry," says the Rabbit. "You can only choose from Table 2."

"Why can't I have the things on Table 1?" you ask, angrily.

"There is a reason," replies the Rabbit, firmly, "but I can't tell you what it is."

"Why not?"

"Because there's no point in telling you. Take whatever you want from Table 2."

You argue for a while but the Rabbit won't yield. You pick up a few boxes from Table 2 and leave. The next day, feeling annoyed, you go back to see the Rabbit.

"Why could I only have things from Table 2? It's not fair!"

The Rabbit shrugs. "Don't blame me. There's a reason why you couldn't have the items on Table 1 and there's nothing I can do about it."

"What's the reason?" you demand to know.

"Okay," says the White Rabbit. "I'll tell you but you won't like it. You couldn't have the things on Table 1 because you didn't choose any of them."

"What do you mean?!" you exclaim. "I *did* choose them. I clearly said I want all the nice things on Table 1!"

The Rabbit calmly explains: "That's not choosing. That's *saying*. There's a big difference. Saying you want something is easy. It takes no effort. Choosing something takes longer — maybe days or weeks. Maybe years. You can't have what you don't choose."

This story is fiction, as you can tell by the fact that it features a talking rabbit. However, in another sense, it's a true story for many people. They *say* they want lots of good things. Saying is easy. But they don't actually *choose* those things. Choosing involves taking the steps that allow the things you want to happen. Choosing is something you *do*, not something you *say*.

You can say you want to be a successful comedian. However, just saying this and practising a bit in front of a mirror is easy. Choosing to be a successful comedian means taking the steps to allow your successful career to happen: writing material, rehearsing, chasing every gig and pursuing every opportunity. It's hard, tiring and frustrating.

You can say you want money. But choosing to have money means taking the necessary steps to allow money to come to you. As I mention elsewhere in this book, it took me five years to create my first e-commerce website.

You can say you want to find the partner of your dreams. But choosing to find your ideal partner means taking the steps that will allow this person to come into your life. This means going out and meeting lots of people until you find him or her.

Saying isn't choosing. What you choose is defined by what you do, not by what you say. It's defined by the steps you take to allow a specific result to occur.

What you choose is up to you.

Table 1 or Table 2?

21. Changes

*"Success and failure are both difficult to endure.
Along with success come drugs, divorce, fornication,
bullying, travel, meditation, medication, depression,
neurosis and suicide. With failure comes failure."*

— Joseph Heller

21. Changes

Change The World

You can change the world.

You don't have to invent anything, break a world record or be on the cover of a magazine. You don't have to be rich or famous, start a political campaign or invent a better mousetrap. All you have to do is choose the right time to say four words:

"I believe in you."

There are many people who could have achieved great things but they never tried. Why not? Because there was nobody there to say, "I believe in you." They could have given us great inventions, started successful companies, written brilliant music, solved important problems or written amazing books. They never did these things because nobody ever offered encouragement or a few words of support.

Very often, the only thing people need in order to start on their path to success is someone to express a little faith in them, to say "I believe in you" or words to that effect.

There are always plenty of voices saying the opposite. The world is never short of doubt, indifference and scorn. Offering someone a simple "I believe in you" can make a big difference. You don't have to do this in a loud or conspicuous way. It can be enough just to be chatting to someone and say, "I think you'd probably be good at that," or, "Sounds like a pretty good plan to me."

However you phrase it, saying "I believe in you" can make a profound difference to someone's life. You don't necessarily have to believe in every aspect of every plan that someone mentions. There may be some things they will need to revise or reconsider later. However, you can usually focus on at least one aspect of someone's dream or goal and find a way to say, "I believe in you."

However you say it, and whoever you say it to, it's a wonderful thing to say. We don't say it to one another nearly often enough.

By doing this, you can change someone's life.

By doing this, you can make the world a much better place.

By doing this, you can make your life much better as well.

Change Yourself

As well as telling other people that you believe in them, I suggest you also believe in yourself.

All your life, there have been people, messages and experiences that clipped your wings, chained your ambition, took away some of the golden potential you *could* feel about yourself. The world is never short of people saying or implying that you're not quite good enough, you're not destined for a great life.

It's very easy to succumb to the brainwashing chorus that says: "Do this boring thing every day because that's all you're good for. Eat this junk food that makes you fat. Watch TV, waste your time. Buy stuff we tell you to buy. It's all you deserve."

All your life, you have been exposed to messages like this, either stated or implied. How's it working out for you?

Here's a different approach you might like to try.

One: love yourself and believe that you're great, with lots of potential. The past is the past and no-one can change it. The future is yours and no-one can *stop* you changing it.

Two: accept that you're entitled to all that is best in life. Good health, fresh and healthy food, fitness, fine friends, true love, material wealth and everything else that is great, good, positive, fun and enjoyable.

Three: accept that not only are you entitled to these things but you can have them. You just have to choose them — not by what you say but by what you do. Think about what you want with the 'allow' attitude rather than the 'get' attitude.

Meditate each day, focusing first on what you want to give to the world and then on what you want the world to give you and the steps you are taking to allow this to happen. You don't have to be a bored worker or a passive consumer if you don't want to be. You can go on your self-employed journey and enjoy every step of the way.

You are great. You are entitled to the best. You can have the best that this life has to offer.

You don't have to believe me and I'm not asking you to. Believe yourself.

Do you have a better alternative?

22. A Bit About Me

"Procrastination is the art of keeping up with yesterday."

— Don Marquis

22. A Bit About Me

My name is Ian and I know a lot about rain. This is because I grew up in the north-west of England, near Manchester. It's a place with a damp climate, warm heart and fifty words for wet.

Since then I've lived in various places and I'm currently based near the wonderful city of London.

Here's my story.

Part 1: Living The Sleep

See if you can spot a pattern here.

When I was young, they said, "There are some important school exams you have to take when you're 16. If you pass them, that's okay. But if you don't, you're a failure."

Being a failure didn't sound great so I tried to pass these exams. This wasn't easy because I'm not intellectually strong. I'm not playing the false modesty card — it's the truth. So I did a stupid amount of homework and burned lots of useless stuff into my head, none of which I can now recall or have ever needed to. To my surprise, I somehow passed the exams.

After I'd passed them, I thought maybe I could feel good about myself. But they said, "No! There are some other important exams you take when you're 18. If you pass them, that's okay. But if you don't, you're a failure."

Being a failure still didn't sound great, so I spent another million hours committing more amazingly useless stuff to memory just long enough to regurgitate it during a three-hour exam. Apparently, this was enough to pass the exams.

I thought maybe now I could feel good about myself. But they said, "No! There's this thing called a degree and it's important that you get one. If you can get a degree, that's okay. But if you don't, you're a failure."

So I went to Sheffield University, which I enjoyed immensely, and started studying for a degree. It was a very embarrassing degree. I don't really want to mention what it was but, in the interests of humility and full disclosure, I will tell you. It was a degree in English Literature and Philosophy.

You might not be aware of how utterly useless this is, so let me explain.

Go to a fast food place or a burger bar. Find one of the bins or trash cans outside. Put your hand in and pull out something at random. Whatever you have in your hand will be worth more than an honours degree in English Literature and Philosophy.

So I got my degree, largely because it was the sort of degree where I would have had to work hard *not* to get it.

I thought maybe by this stage I was allowed to feel good about myself. But they said, "No! What matters is whether you can get a job. If you can get a job, that's okay. But if you can't, you're a failure."

So I got a job. Then they said, "Ah, but what matters is whether you can get a *better* job. One that pays you more money so you can buy more stuff!"

I said, "What stuff? Look, I've got a really nice guitar, I can make myself a cup of tea whenever I want and the local library has lots of great books in it. To be honest, I'm kind of happy where I am and I don't think I need more stuff."

They said, "You don't understand! You've got to get a better job to earn more money to buy more stuff! Don't argue! If you can get a better job, that's okay. But if you can't, you're a failure."

So I got a better job.

I thought maybe I could, at long last, feel good about myself. But they said, "No! What matters is, can you get into management? Because if you can, that's okay. But if you can't, you're a failure."

So I got into management.

Then they said, "Ah! But what matters is, can you get into senior management? Because if you can, that's okay. But if you can't, you're a failure."

So I got into senior management. I ended up as the UK Head of Sales & Marketing for a big, multinational internet technologies company.

Then, in 1997, something happened. I took a good look at my desk, my office, my life, my world. I realised I'd been told I was living the dream but I was actually living the sleep.

So I **woke up**.

Part 2: What Are You Going To Do?

I realised that I wasn't happy.

I realised that I didn't want to go into the Monday management meeting and the Wednesday planning meeting and the Friday team meeting. The meetings were dull and they never seemed to achieve anything either.

Every day, I was doing things the way other people told me I had to do them — even when their ideas suggested a passionate commitment to corporate suicide. I felt like I was always moving in slow motion, wearing the heavy, lead-lined diving boots of a life lived without imagination. I was also *really* bored.

I wanted to live my life for me instead of following other people's ideas about how I should spend my time. So I just walked out.

I said, "I've had enough. It's boring and I want more than this to look back on."

People said, "Is this a mid-life crisis?"

I was in my thirties. I said, "No, it's called waking up."

People said, "What are you going to do?"

I said, "I'm not really sure but it has to be more interesting than this."

People said, "How will you survive?"

I looked around the office and I said, "Do you call this surviving? This isn't surviving. It's existing. Anyway, I don't want to survive. I want to live."

People said, "Oh, it's very brave of you to do your own thing and leave behind the big salary, the company car and all the perks."

I said, "The way I see it, the brave people are the ones who can look ahead and see more of the same — the commuting, the meetings, the spreadsheets, the wretched company parties — and go forward into that tunnel. I can't do that. It's just too scary to think that's all I will have to look back on."

So I left my job and I went on an adventure called 'Seeing what happens next'. It's been a pretty good adventure, to be honest. I'm still on it and I love every minute of it.

Part 3: The Adventure Goes On

After I'd walked out of my job, I tried various things — a bit of freelance writing here, some marketing work there.

I also decided to write a book about cold reading. I offered it to various publishers and in their infinite wisdom they said no, there's no market for it, there's no point, you're wasting your time, don't bother.

By rejecting my book these talented professionals did me a wonderful favour. I taught myself how to self-publish the book and how to sell it online. So far I've sold over 50,000 copies to customers in more than 60 countries and it just keeps selling and selling, even though I've never spent a penny on advertising of any kind.

What else have I done apart from write a mildly popular book on cold reading?

My great passion is travelling and travel photography. I've seen the sun both rise and set over Ayer's Rock and explored the incredible stone city of Petra in Jordan. I've enjoyed the view from the very top of the Petronas Towers and explored the depths of the amazing Postojna Caves in Slovenia. I've visited the unbelievably beautiful town of Baden-Baden, journeyed along Australia's Gold Coast, visited Tivoli in Copenhagen at Christmas and walked the roof of Il Duomo in Milan.

I've taken a hot-air balloon ride at dawn over the mountains of Cappadocia and stayed at the amazing Hotel zum Zauberkabinett in Bavaria. I've been inside the incredible Cabazon dinosaurs, seen the glassmakers of Murano and taken a 10m trek through Repovesi National Park in Finland.

I've seen the Cathedral on Spilled Blood in St. Petersburg and the Kiyomitzu temple of Kyoto — built from wood but without using nails or tools. I've been inside the awesome Turning Torso of Malmo and stood next to the full-size Saturn V rocket at Kennedy Space Centre. I've climbed the Leaning Tower of Pisa, sat in a jail cell in Alcatraz, flown a helicopter over Sydney harbour and been to Vienna to see my favourite painting: Breughel's 'Return Of The Hunters'.

I've met scores of fascinating people all over the world. Some of them are famous and I could drop a few names but I won't. Others may not be famous but they are wonderful and incredible people all the same.

I'm neither rich nor famous but I do have a very enjoyable and fulfilling life. I've lectured by invitation at both Oxford and Cambridge. I've performed just about everywhere, including places where they don't normally have performers, such as the Times Literary Festival. I was hired by the FBI to teach their agents. I lectured by invitation to the sports psychologists of the British Olympics team and I've also been an advisor to the Ministry of Defence. I've taken part in some extraordinary events such as the STTAR Summit in Philadelphia and the Human Hacking conference in Orlando. Luckily, I've sometimes been invited to lecture and perform at magic conventions, including 'Magic Live' in Las Vegas and the Blackpool Magic Convention (the largest such convention in the world).

I am lucky enough to have plenty of love in my life. If life has taught me anything, it's that love is what makes everything else make sense.

Most of all, I've had fun.

I've done all these things just by waking up.

If you went on a similar adventure, you wouldn't do the same things or go down the same paths as me. But I expect you would have just as much fun.

I'm happy to say that most of my friends and many of my clients are self-employed people. I love them all, and greatly admire their creativity, achievements, talent, hard work and laughter.

Life is good.

Final Words

Thank you for reading 'How To Work For Yourself And Win'. I hope that you found it useful.

Maybe you and I will one day meet either online or in real life. I look forward to it! Even if that never happens, I nonetheless wish you all the luck and success in the world.

If you want to get in touch, I'd love to hear from you. Feel free to send me an email (ian@ianrowland.com or visit any of my websites and use the email link provided).

— Ian Rowland

London, 2020

---

www.ianrowland.com
About my work as a writer-for-hire.

www.coldreadingsuccess.com
Everything to do with cold reading and 'cold reading for business'.

www.ianrowlandtraining.com
My talks and training for conferences, corporate groups and private clients.

End Note 1: An Invitation

Let's Work Together!

Would you like me to help you to work for yourself, build your career and achieve your goals?

You can hire me! I help people all the time via Skype or Zoom. For details see www.ianrowland.com .

I also give talks, training and keynotes about working for yourself, doing your own thing and living life to the full. Why not hire me to give a talk at your next conference? What could be more worthwhile than helping everyone to work for themselves and live a fulfilled life?

I'd love to work with you. Let me help you to work for yourself and win.

— Ian Rowland

www.ianrowland.com
www.coldreadingsuccess.com
www.ianrowlandtraining.com

End Note 2: Three Requests

Please Help Me If You Can

If you'd like to support me and my work, please tell all your friends about this book and my various websites. I'm self-employed and promote my work as best I can, but a little help is always welcome. If you can help me to 'spread the word', I would be very grateful.

For example, you can mention me to your friends in real life or on social media. Wherever people are discussing self-employment, building their own career, pursuing their goals and dreams, please give me and my books a mention and pass on the link:
www.ianrowland.com

Got contacts in broadcast or online media? Tell them about me or about this book. They might get a good story, article or feature out of it — if you've got an audience, I've got content! Maybe you can help me to get media appearances or to get booked to give a talk or presentation. I'd appreciate whatever help you want to offer. I want to help people to work for themselves and win. Thank you for any assistance you can give me.

Improvements, Fixes And Flubs

If you have notes or ideas about how I can improve this book, or if you've noticed errors I should fix, I'd love to hear from you. If there are factual errors, things I should explain more clearly or typos, I'd love to correct them.

Please Send Me Your Review

Reviews are really helpful. If you can, please send me a review of this book that I can add to the product page on my website. My email address is ian@ianrowland.com . Your review can be published under your own name or can be as anonymous as you wish.

Your review doesn't have to very long or a literary masterpiece. Short reviews can be great although if you *want* to write a detailed review then you're welcome to do so! Also, don't worry if your writing needs a little help or tidying up. I can take care of that for you.

You can also submit reviews to Amazon if you obtained any of my books from there.

What Can I Do For You?

Personal Coaching And Training

I work with private clients all over the world, either in person or via the internet. Some people contact me for help with weight loss and fitness. Others want a little help with areas such as self-fulfilment and personal success, building their business, creating a passive income or related subjects. Let's work together and see what value I can provide for you!

See any of my websites for details.

Talks, Keynotes And Corporate Training

I love taking part in live events! I offer excellent talks, training and keynotes on subjects such as persuasion and communication skills, working for yourself, creating digital products and building a passive income. I often add touches of magic and mindreading, just to make my sessions a little bit different!

To date, I've worked for the FBI, Google, Coca-Cola, Marks & Spencer, The British Olympics Team, The Ministry of Defence, Hewlett-Packard, The Philadelphia 76ers, CapGemini, BBC, Kier Construction, NBC, The Crown Estate, Iceland, Medtronic, Unilever, The Sunday Times Oxford Literary Festival, The Prince's Charities, McKinsey & Company, Eurostar Software Testing Conference, Ogilvy & Mather, Rabobank, London Business School, ABC Television, Channel 4, Cambridge Technology Partners, Synon, Valtech and many other companies.

I've also lectured at Oxford University, Cambridge University, the California Institute of Technology and Monash University.

Writing

A friend once described me as 'a book midwife'. If you have a book in you, I'll help you to write it, publish it yourself, market it and make some money from it. I've been a professional writer for over 35 years and I offer a complete, end-to-end service.

I particularly like helping people to create a passive income for themselves: create a product, set up a website, make money while you sleep. This is what I've been doing for about twenty years. I can guide you through the entire process! It's a challenging road to travel, to be sure, but at the same time highly satisfying and rewarding.

Social Media

I'd love to stay in touch via social media!

For each of my main websites, there is a corresponding Facebook page:

www.ianrowland.com
www.coldreadingsuccess.com
www.ianrowlandtraining.com

You can also find me on:
Twitter (@IanRowland1)
Linked In
Instagram

Some Kind Words...

"My FBI Behavioural Analysis Program hired Ian to work with and train our team for a full day. He demonstrated and taught us a lot about cold reading and how we could apply it to our work as behavioural analysts. In addition, he covered advanced communication skills, persuasive language and relevant insights into the art of 'misdirection'. At the conclusion of his comprehensive seminar, he entertained our entire team and families with a mindreading show at an evening social. Not only was it great fun, but even today my team is still talking about it. I'd highly recommend Ian to anyone who's interested in these subjects and wants a first-class speaker and trainer."
— *Robin Dreeke, former Special Agent and Head of **FBI Behavioural Analysis Program***

"I regard Ian as a first-rate trainer and consultant. He has amazing material, he always delivers and he's great to work with."
— *A. Sanghi, Lead Economist, **World Bank Group***

"Ian has a very engaging and energising style and he was thought-provoking and entertaining throughout. Most importantly, everyone said it was a great use of their time. Ian gave us plenty of ways to work smarter and be more effective both professionally and personally."
— *A. Mellor, **Marks & Spencer***

"Ian is the best speaker and trainer I've ever seen and he hosted our day perfectly. We learned a lot, he was entertaining and I know we'll be more successful this year thanks to what he shared with us."
— *D. Holmes, Financial Director, **Healthcare Learning***

"We had some of the top experts around the globe in their field, but when we looked at how people were registering for the conference and what the attendees wanted, overwhelmingly we saw very large numbers signing up for Ian's course, so much so that his class was the largest in the whole session that we had for those three days."
— *Chris Hadnagy, **Organiser, Human Hacking Conference***

"Of the hundred plus lectures and shows we have hosted at Caltech none have brought more enthusiastic praise than your performance. I have now heard from dozens of people in the audience, all of whom said this was one of the most entertaining, informative, and above all *funny* shows they had ever seen. You are to be congratulated for breathing so much life and class into the science and skeptics community."
— *Michael Shermer, **Executive Director, Skeptics Society***

"Ian's special talent lies in his ability to communicate useful information about self-improvement, business, psychology and, yes, magic to diverse audiences around the world. His books are essential reading and if you get the opportunity to hear him speak, don't miss him! For those outside the world of magic and mindreading, let me tell you that Ian is very highly regarded in the trade. He even gets hired to go to major conventions and teach other magicians! When I was Editor of the Magic Circle's magazine, I asked Ian to write a column on mindreading, which he did for 12 years to great acclaim."
— *Matthew Field*, **Member of the Inner Magic Circle**

"I've been an Independent Financial Advisor for 20 years and have learned from people like Dale Carnegie, Anthony Robbins, Jim Rohn and Brian Tracy. I now include Ian Rowland on that list. Having attended his courses and invested in some personal coaching with him, I cannot recommend him highly enough. His unique insights regarding positive persuasion and what makes people tick will prove invaluable in your personal and business life. He's funny, engaging and a leader in his field."
— *Mike LeGassick*, **Leading Independent Financial Advisor**, UK

"I make it my business to learn from experts. I spent four days with Ian and we covered a range of skills that I know will help me both personally and professionally — particularly inter-personal skills and ways to establish instant rapport with people. I think he's terrific."
— *Sam Q.*, **Entrepreneur**, Saudi Arabia

"I'm a sales guy. I've studied all the big names and been trained by some of the best in the business. I trained with Ian via Skype and he just blew my mind with techniques and perspectives I never knew before. It's all practical. I use what Ian taught me almost every day. He opened my eyes to aspects of communication that truly deserve the term 'magic'."
— *Michael Martin*, **Sales professional**, USA

"I studied Cold Reading For Business with Ian via Skype and without doubt it's my best investment this year! Ian is an excellent teacher and working with him is very enjoyable. In addition, Ian is incredibly generous with his knowledge in many adjacent fields.
— *Patrick Ehrich*, **Teacher and Educational Trainer**, Germany

Love And Gratitude

This book was created entirely by self-employed people!

I wrote the book, knocked up the cover and published it.

For proofreading, I turned to the very thorough and reliable Nicole Oppler, who works for herself as a proofreader and copy editor. She did a superb job for me and did it very quickly!

Laylah Perrin helped me with the cover design and a few technical issues I couldn't resolve for myself. She is a superb graphic designer who has handled several assignments for me in recent years.

A number of my self-employed friends saw early drafts of this book and helped me with comments, criticisms and suggestions. I would therefore like to thank: Peter Bryant, Patrick Ehrich, Mark Elsdon, Matthew Field, Anja Geist, Andy Gibney, Gilan Gork, Jessie Haag, Lee Hathaway, John Holt, Lynne Kelly, Ian Kendall, Marika Rauscher, Abbie Hirst, Rory Raven and Di Sweeney.

Di gets a second mention because she also kept me supplied with excellent baked goods while I was working on this book. She makes the best cherry and coconut loaf in the world!

Lee Hathaway also gets a second mention because he's the single most useful and helpful person to know in the entire universe. One way or another, with all his knowledge and contacts, Lee has helped me with every aspect of this project.

I also want to thank all my brilliant and talented friends in the world of magic and the allied arts. Thank you for being so amazingly impressive, for always being so willing to help and for all the good times shared. The worldwide magic community is very dear to my heart and has made a huge difference to my life and to my self-employment journey. May there be many more good times to come!

Many other friends made contributions both large and small. James Batchelor, my personal business guru, has been endlessly supportive with good ideas and advice, as always. My very long and detailed discussions with Dr. Sam Qurashi helped me to crystallise many of the ideas featured in these pages.

Liam O'Neill provided a great deal of inspiration and also kept me fuelled with a home-made batch of '15s'. Gary Turner is another great source of inspiration.

My good friends AJ Green and Julia Cotterill supported and helped me in numerous ways during the gestation of this book, not least by being reliably available for a coffee or a night out whenever I felt like it! I'd also like to thank James Pritchard for all the good times and wonderfully funny conversations we've shared.

Experienced writer and journalist Charlie Burgess offered very helpful constructive criticism and advised me on the best title to use for the book. Jaq Greenspon was also very helpful and has often helped me with research and sources.

I also wish to thank Chris Hadnagy, Dov Baron, Wes Schaeffer, Chase Hughes and Robin Dreeke, Stephanie Paul and Brittney Caldwell for help, advice, assistance and good times shared.

If I have left out anyone I ought to have thanked, please accept my sincere apologies. If I tried to include everyone to whom I owe a debt of gratitude, I'd need another hundred pages.

— Ian

London, 2020

"A friend may well be reckoned the masterpiece of Nature."
— R. W. Emerson

Printed in the USA
CPSIA information can be obtained
at www.ICGtesting.com
LVHW011800180923
758543LV00009B/309